4 Colors / One Image

Mattias Nyman

Peachpit Press
Berkeley, California

4 Colors / One Image

Mattias Nyman

translated by Everett M. Ellestad / INTENSE AB

Originally published in Sweden by Software Plus Scandinavia AB

Copyright © 1991, 1993 Mattias Nyman / Software Plus Scandinavia AB

Copyright © 1993 Mattias Nyman / Peachpit Press

Peachpit Press, Inc.

2414 Sixth Street

Berkeley, CA 94710

510/548-4393

510/548-5991

Graphic design and production: Mattias Nyman, Tom Serianni

Cover design: Ted Mader + Associates

Illustrations: John Dranger, Anders Blomberg / ElectroPix, Anders F. Rönnblom / Studio Matchbox

ISBN: 1-56609-083-0

Printed and bound in Sweden

Printing	*2*
Screens	*3*
Resolution	*6*
Color Systems	*10*
Tonal Range	*14*
Scanner	*16*
Original Types	*18*
File Formats	*20*
Proofs	*22*
Calibration	*24*
Scanning	*26*
Tone Correction	*28*
Color Correction	*30*
Separation	*34*
Image Manipulation	*38*
Duplex	*44*
Tonal Value Changes	*46*
Sharpening Filters	*50*
Image Compression	*52*
Trapping	*54*
Output	*56*
Calibration	*58*
Black & White	*60*
Color Images	*62*
Color Correction	*66*
Background Stripping	*70*
Tonal Value Changes	*73*

CONTENTS

Introduction

4 Colors/One Image explores two fields in the graphic arts: color reproduction and electronic image manipulation. The distinction between the two is often ambiguous, however. How much can skin tone be altered to make it look better in print before you start changing "reality"? Is removing the background around an object (a person, for instance) considered a standard layout procedure, or does it manipulate the image enough to change its context?

Since most desktop publishers working with color images are faced with the deceptively simple task of reproducing an image as close to the original as possible, this book concentrates on straightforward color reproduction techniques. After you've mastered these basic procedures, you can move on to the almost limitless creative possibilities found in image retouching and manipulation.

The focus of this book is on producing high-quality color output in a desktop publishing environment. The book has been divided into three parts: green, red and blue. The green section covers the basics of color theory; the red applies theory to real-world examples using Photoshop and Cachet; the blue section shows step-by-step procedures for accomplishing specific tasks, such as scanning and color correction.

Frequently, several different methods and procedures are available that will ultimately produce the same result. Some of these varying techniques are explored and illustrated here. Only you, as the end user, can decided which methods are most appropriate for your specific needs and projects.

I sincerely hope this book is useful in increasing your understanding of the powerful, state-of-the-art tools available for electronic pre-press four-color imaging.

Mattias Nyman
July, 1993
Stockholm, Sweden

A NUMBER OF DIFFERENT printing processes exist for transferring images onto paper. A few of them are letterpress, lithography, gravure and screen (also called silk-screen). The most common process nowadays is a litho process usually known as offset.

In the offset process, the original image is transferred onto a printing plate attached to the plate cylinder of the press. The image areas of the plate are treated to become hydrophobic and the nonprinting areas are made hydrophilic. Water and ink are then applied to the cylinder. The greasy ink adheres to the hydrophobic surfaces and the water keeps the non-image surfaces ink-free. In the next step, the image is transferred onto a rubber blanket wrapped around another cylinder. Finally, the image is printed onto the paper that is fed between the blanket cylinder and an impression cylinder.

For multi-color printing—four color, for example—the paper has to pass through as many presses as there are colors. Either each color is allowed to dry before being fed into the next press, or all of the colors are printed onto the paper in rapid succession, called wet-on-wet.

The paper is normally run through the presses in two different ways: either sheet-fed or web-fed. Web-fed offset, where the paper runs off a reel of paper, is the most common method for printing newspapers and catalogs. Sheet-fed offset is most commonly used for high quality printing.

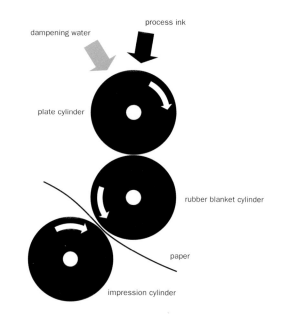

FIG 2 The offset litho process. Process ink and water are applied to a plate attached to a cylinder. The plate presses against a rubber blanket wrapped around another cylinder. The image transferred to the rubber blanket is, in turn, transferred to the paper fed between the rubber blanket cylinder and the impression cylinder.

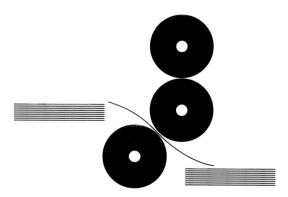

FIG 3 In sheet-fed offset printing, paper is fed from a stack of individual sheets.

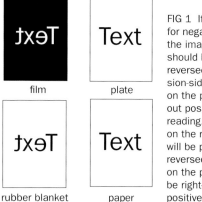

film

plate

rubber blanket

paper

FIG 1 If an offset plate for negative film is used, the image on the film should be negative and reversed with the emulsion-side up. The image on the plate will come out positive and right-reading. The image on the rubber blanket will be positive and reversed. The image on the paper will then be right-reading and positive.

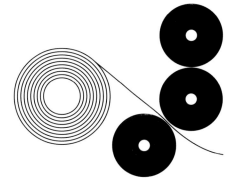

FIG 4 In web-fed offset printing, the paper is fed from a reel.

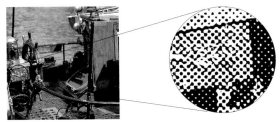

FIG 5 The small halftone dots create an optical illusion of a continuous-tone image.

FIG 6 Four separate screened images in the four process inks: cyan, magenta, yellow and black, or **CMYK** for short. Together, they create a complete range of color.

REPRODUCTION IS THE process of transferring an original photo or illustration onto a printing plate. This is primarily done in two stages: first, a halftone image is produced on transparent photographic film. This film is then contact-copied onto the printing plate.

Since offset litho is a binary process—either ink is printed on the paper or it is not—the countless gray shades or color tones of the original must be simulated in some way. This is done by halftone screening. The image is differentiated into a number of dots of varying sizes, each corresponding to the various tones of the original. The many dots create an illusion of a continuous tone image.

Printed color images are built up of four separate screen images, one for each process ink color: cyan, magenta, yellow and black. Theoretically, the first three should be enough, but these colors have certain deficiencies that make it difficult to produce a true black. Black is used to produce good contrast.

Screen frequency (also referred to as screen ruling) is a measure of the proximity of the centers of the dots. The higher the frequency, the finer the screen and the better the reproduced continuous tone image. The frequency cannot be too great, however, since the dots will tend to run together on paper. The result is a reduction in contrast range: the image becomes darker, and details in the darker areas of the image disappear.

Whether a coarse or fine screen should be used depends on the quality of the paper and the printing process. Paper manufacturers can often recommend a suitable screen frequency. The tonal range of the original also affects the choice of screen frequency. A light original that is printed on coated paper in a sheet-fed offset press can be screened with a higher frequency than a dark original that is printed on newspaper in a web-fed press.

When printing color images, all the colors (except the one printed first) are partially printed on top of one another. In order to ensure that as much ink as possible is printed directly on the paper, the various screens are given different angles. It is important that the correct angle be used. If not, a moiré pattern may result that will adversely affect the quality of the image.

Figure 7 shows some commonly used screen angles. Various screen angle combinations can be used, depending on the dominant image color. The dominant color is printed at the best angle: 45 degrees, which is the angle least visible to the eye. In separation processes currently used, it is usually the black separation that is dominant.

A round halftone dot is most often used, but other shapes are available: elliptical, square and line halftone screens are a few of the most common. The elliptical dot produces smoother color transitions, but also larger dot gain during printing. Line screens are used for special effects.

All electronic reproduction work uses digital halftone screens. Digital halftones are built up of small square matrices, and therefore cannot be rotated to any angle in all screen frequencies. The fact that it may not be possible to choose exactly the desired angle and frequency may create moiré patterns. To solve this problem, three principle halftone screen systems have been introduced on the PostScript market: Agfa Balanced Screening Technology (ABS), Adobe Accurate Screening, and HQS Screening from Linotype-Hell. These systems all produce excellent results, and help avoid moiré patterns.

The halftone screen to be used depends on the output. Linotronic's imagesetter uses HQS, while Agfa's uses ABS and output devices compatible with PostScript Level 2 use Adobe Accurate Screening.

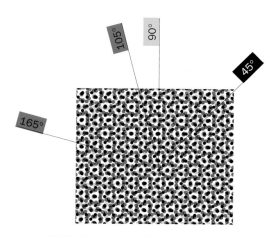

FIG 7 An example of a common combination of screen angles. Since yellow is the weakest color, it is placed only 15 degrees from cyan. All other colors are separated by at least 45 degrees.

FIG 8 If incorrect screen angles are used, an interference, or moiré, pattern will be created. This can be seen as square-like patterns in the photo.

FIG 9 For this photo, a screen frequency of 75 lpi was used.

Halftone settings can be stored along with the image file, which is stored in EPS or DCS format. Most often these settings are not necessary; instead, the RIP defines the screen angles and frequency. One reason to store halftone settings would be to have varying screen frequencies and angles appear on the same page.

In Adobe Photoshop, the halftone settings can be adjusted using the *Screens* dialog box, which is found under the button of the same name in the *Page Setup* dialog box. In Cachet, this is done when saving separations or during output by using the dialog box found under the *Halftone* button.

FIG 10 For this photo, a screen frequency of 120 lpi was used.

Recommended screen frequencies for offset printing

Lines per inch (lpi)	Suitable for
75–85	Newspaper, board
100	Wood-free paper, coated wood-containing paper
133–150	Coated paper
150–200	Art paper or double-coated paper

FIG 11 For this photo, a screen frequency of 150 lpi was used.

RIP
This is an abbreviation for Raster Image Processor — the machine that transforms DTP program instructions, stored in PostScript language, into language the imagesetting equipment can understand.

PostScript
This is a page description language used to describe how a page is built up of various objects (copy, lines, images). It is becoming the *de facto* standard in the graphics industry.

WHEN AN ORIGINAL is scanned and stored in a computer, it is transformed into pixels. The scanning resolution is defined as the number of pixels per unit of length, e.g. inches or centimeters.

As long as the number of pixels is constant, the file size remains constant. The resolution can, however, be altered. If it is reduced, the result will be an image that is larger in area, but the file size will remain the same as before. This corresponds to enlarging the image. In other words, the resolution defines only the number of pixels per unit of length.

During output, the image is built up of a number of halftone dots. In order for the transformation from pixels to halftone dots to be the best possible, there must be four times as many pixels as halftone dots, which is to say that the resolution is twice as high as the screen frequency ($2 \cdot 2 = 4$). The resolution multiplied by the enlargement factor will then provide the necessary scanning resolution.

The doubling of the screen frequency is derived from the "sampling theory." The sampling factor can, however, be reduced from 2 to 1.5, or even lower, if a certain loss of sharpness and detail is acceptable.

If the screen frequency and file size have been set, the latter can be adjusted so that the resolution will not be more than twice the screen frequency. If the resolution is greater, the file size will be greater, and it will take more time to work with, and print out, the image.

The halftone dots of the image are built up of small machine spots produced by the image-setter. A halftone dot consists of a varying number of machine spots, depending on its size. The number of machine spots per unit of length is called output resolution.

FIG 12 The original photo contains a continuous-tone image. It is neither screened nor divided into pixels.
(It is screened here in order for it to be printed.)

FIG 13 When an image is scanned by the computer, it is divided up into small square pixels. The number of pixels per unit of length is determined by the scanner's resolution.

FIG 14 When the image is screened, four pixels are analyzed. The average value of these four pixels determines the size of the corresponding halftone dot.

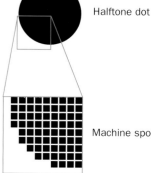

Halftone dot

Machine spot

FIG 15 A halftone dot is built up of several small machine spots. The size of these machine spots is determined by the output resolution.

Pixel
This is an abbreviation of picture element and constitutes the smallest element of a scanned image. Each pixel is a square that is assigned a color or a gray value.

FIG 16 Here, the sampling factor is 1—the scanning resolution is the same as the screen frequency. In this case, it is 150 lpi.

FIG 17 Here, the sampling factor is 1.5. The scanning resolution is therefore 225 dpi, and the screen frequency is 150 lpi.

FIG 18 Here, the sampling factor is 2 (the ideal ratio between scanning resolution and screen frequency). The scanning resolution is 300 dpi, and the screen frequency is 150 lpi.

The output resolution often cannot be altered much. There are two common fixed resolutions: one close to 1200 dpi, and another around 2400 dpi. Choosing one depends on the screen frequency used. To reproduce a four-color image, there needs to be four separate halftones. Each halftone image, one for each process ink, contains a maximum of 256 shades of gray. For these to be reproduced with a set screen frequency, the imagesetter must have a certain resolution.

$$\left(\frac{\text{output resolution}}{\text{screen frequency}}\right)^2 + 1 = \begin{array}{l}\text{number of gray}\\ \text{shades (levels)}\end{array}$$

FIG 19 Use this fomula to calculate how many shades of gray can be reproduced for a set output resolution and screen frequency. Below are some examples of how it is used.

$$\left(\frac{2\,400}{133}\right)^2 + 1 = 325 > 256$$

EXAMPLE 1 An output resolution of 2400 dpi and a screen frequency of 133 lpi will give 325 possible gray shades. This is sufficient for reproducing the 256 shades of gray found in the scanned image.

$$\left(\frac{1\,200}{75}\right)^2 + 1 = 257 > 256$$

EXAMPLE 2 An output resolution of 1200 dpi and a screen frequency of 75 lpi will give 257 possible gray shades—almost exactly as many as found in the scanned image.

$$\left(\frac{1\,270}{85}\right)^2 + 1 = 224 \text{ (acceptable)}$$

EXAMPLE 3 A common combination is an output resolution of 1270 dpi and a screen frequency of 85 lpi. The result, 224 gray shades, is acceptable, since it is close to the 256 gray shades in the image.

FIG 20 Use this fomula to determine how high the scanning resolution must be, when the size of the original and the size of the printed image are known.

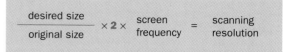

$$\frac{\text{desired size}}{\text{original size}} \times 2 \times \begin{array}{l}\text{screen}\\ \text{frequency}\end{array} = \begin{array}{l}\text{scanning}\\ \text{resolution}\end{array}$$

FIG 21 To determine how large an image can be printed, use this formula when the number of pixels along one side is known. (If you multiple by 25.4, the result will be in millimeters.)

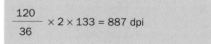

$$\frac{\text{number of pixels}}{2 \times \text{screen frequency}} = \text{image size in inches}$$

The red digit 2 is derived from the sampling theory. If a certain loss of quality is acceptable, this factor can be reduced to 1.5. In most cases, there will be no noticeable difference (see page 7).

EXAMPLE 4 To print an image 120 mm wide from a small slide (24 x 36 mm), using a screen frequency of 133 lpi, calculate:

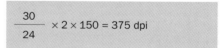

$$\frac{120}{36} \times 2 \times 133 = 887 \text{ dpi}$$

Set to scan with a resolution of at least 887 dpi.

EXAMPLE 5 To print an image 30 cm high from a photo measuring 18 x 24 cm, with a screen frequency of 150 lpi, calculate:

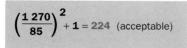

$$\frac{30}{24} \times 2 \times 150 = 375 \text{ dpi}$$

Set to scan with a resolution of at least 375 dpi.

EXAMPLE 6 The photo is 1024 pixels high and the screen frequency is 85 lpi. To find out how high an image can be printed, calculate:

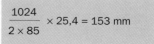

$$\frac{1024}{2 \times 85} \times 25{,}4 = 153 \text{ mm}$$

The image can be 153 mm high using a sampling factor of 2. If the sampling factor is reduced, the image can be larger.

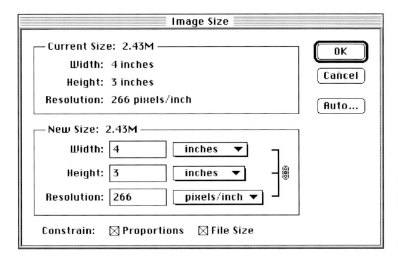

FIG 22 This shows the *Image Size* dialog box from Adobe Photoshop The image has been scanned using a resolution of 266 dpi, because the intended screen frequency is 133 lpi. The original is 3 in. high by 4 in. wide.

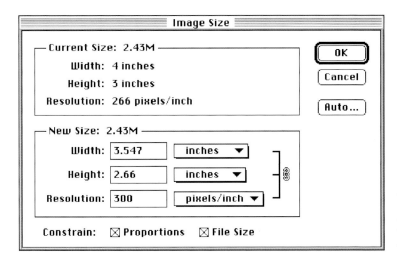

FIG 23 The resolution is altered to 300 dpi, in order to match a screen frequency of 150 lpi. The image can be made 2.66 in. high by 3.547 in. wide, if the sampling factor is to be 2. The number of pixels is the same as in the previous figure.

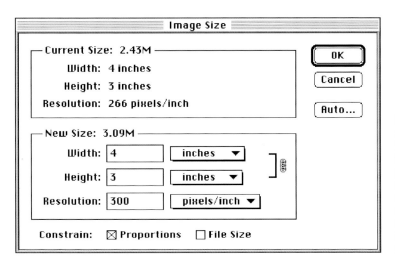

FIG 24 Here, the number of pixels are altered so the resolution and size of the image will be the same. The result is that the file size increases. The new pixels forming the image are created artificially by analyzing the adjacent pixels. The quality of this image will not be as good as if it had been scanned with a resolution of 300 dpi from the start. In that case, no new pixels would have had to be artificially created.

OR COLOR REPRODUCTION in a DTP environment, there are three different systems used to describe color. The additive and subtractive systems describe a color's relative composition of three primary colors. The third system, the CIE system, is an absolute system, in which a particular color is assigned three numerical coordinates in a color model.

The additive color system uses combinations of red, green and blue to produce all the colors of the spectrum. (Equal parts of red, green and blue light create white light.) This is the system that is used for scanning an image and reproducing it on a monitor. The intensity of minute red, green and blue dots on the monitor is varied electronically to build up an image. The additive color system also represents a good method for measuring how the eye sees colors. It is usually called the RGB model, taken from the first letters of each primary color.

The subtractive color system uses cyan, magenta and yellow. Mixing these colors in near-equal parts creates black. This system is the foundation of the art of printing. Cyan, magenta and yellow are called process colors. In Europe, they are defined as the Euroscale. In the U.S.A., they are defined according to SWOP standards. These two definitions are somewhat different, especially regarding cyan.

The most serious fault of the subtractive system is that 100% of cyan, magenta and yellow do not produce a true, solid black, but rather a dark brown. For this reason, black is added in practice, and the system is thus called CMYK (K stands for Key Color).

In both the additive and the subtractive color systems, the numerical definitions of the colors depend on the properties and appearances of the primary colors used. For example, a particular color that is composed of 20% red, 30% green and 50% blue will appear somewhat different depending on how the red, green and blue primaries actually look. Such a difference can be found, for instance, between two different monitor screens.

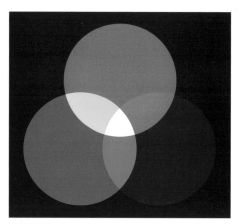

FIG 25 In the additive color system, red, green and blue are the primary colors, and cyan, magenta and yellow are the secondary colors. Red, green and blue together produce white.

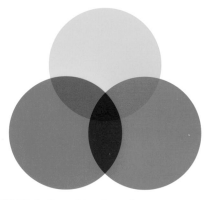

FIG 26 In the subtractive color system, cyan, magenta and yellow are the primary colors, and red, green and blue are the secondary colors. Cyan, magenta and yellow produce black.

Tertiary Colors
These are colors built up of components of all three process colors. Most of the colors in an image are tertiary colors.

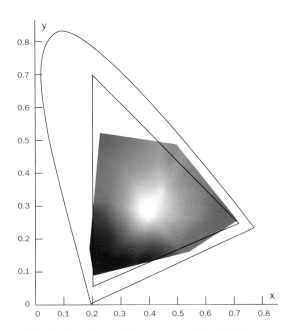

FIG 27 The chromaticity diagram of the CIEXYZ system. The color area represents the colors that can be printed on coated paper. The black triangle encompasses the colors that can be reproduced on a monitor. The outer curved line encompasses colors the eye can see. (Colors in the illustration are approximate.)

FIG 28 Red, green and blue, the three primary colors, have the following coordinates in the chromaticity diagram, which correspond to the stated wavelengths.

	R	G	B
x	0.72	0.28	0.18
y	0.27	0.72	0.08
λ	700	546.1	435.8 (nm)

FIG 29 The European process inks have been assigned the following coordinates in the CIE system.

	C	M	Y
x	0.153	0.464	0.437
y	0.196	0.232	0.494
Y	21.9	17.1	77.8

The actual color coordinates of the inks also depend on what they are to be used for. Inks for newsprint differ substantially from those intended for better paper qualities. Even the process inks from different manufacturers vary. How RGB data are converted to CMYK data, is determined by the parameters for process inks entered into the separation program used.

Other color standards exist—for instance, the American SWOP, in which colors have been assigned other coordinates.

It is advantageous to have a color system with primaries that are standardized and fixed. Such a standardized descriptive color system is the CIEXYZ system. This is a system in which the three basic colors (red, green and blue) have been systematically chosen, and assigned special coordinates. They therefore constitute fixed points in the system.

In a CIE system, all pure hues are plotted along a curve in the x-y plane. Perpendicular to this surface is a Y-axis representing lightness of color, with greater lightness toward the top.

A variation of the CIEXYZ system is called CIELAB. It is designed to be perceptually uniform—that is, equal movements within the color space are perceived by the eye as equal differences in color. This is not the case with the original CIEXYZ system.

In both the RGB system and the CMYK system, there are limitations as to what colors can be reproduced. Unfortunately, the reproducible colors vary for the two systems. This causes difficulties when a color image is to be converted from one system to the other. Some colors simply cannot be reproduced in both systems, and must therefore be approximated by some adjacent color.

If a CIE system is used as a basis for all conversion calculations, it is possible to take the various properties of (for example) the scanner, monitor screen, color printer and process inks into consideration. Examples of such properties are the type of phosphor used in the monitor, the hue error (or contaminant color) of the process inks, and the density of the printer's colors.

In order for the colors displayed on the screen to match the printed colors as closely as possible, it is important that all the components of the system be calibrated and finely tuned.

The deficiencies of the colors in the CMYK system have created a need for a general color correction of images. Impurities in the process inks, and deficiencies in separation filter transmission and absorption, bring about contaminant colors that must be compensated for. Yellow is, for the most part, correct. Cyan, on the other hand, contains a considerable amount of magenta and a smaller amount of yellow. Magenta has someyellow and a small trace of cyan.

Furthermore, color correction may be necessary to remove color tinges found in the original, or simply to change the appearance of the image compared with the original. Frequently, there is a desire to make an illustration more attractive than the original—such as make the grass greener, or the sky bluer.

The most important colors in an image are the so-called memory colors, colors that we easily recognize, and object to if they are wrong. Typical examples are skin colors, grass greens and orange oranges. It is necessary to do color corrections that make these colors look right.

For optimal reproduction of most colors, a high-gloss paper with a high whiteness and smoothness is best. The legibility of black letters is, however, highest on a paper with a slightly uneven surface structure, and a somewhat yellow hue. This means the choice of paper for printed matter containing both words and images is always a compromise. In addition, other factors such as availability, finances and graphic design affect the choice of paper. The adaptability of the reproduction process makes the choice of paper easier.

FIG 30 Color tinges show up as faint, undesirable hues throughout the entire photo. Color tinges can occur if the lighting conditions are wrong for the type of film used. Most slide films tend to produce faint color tinges that vary from film to film.

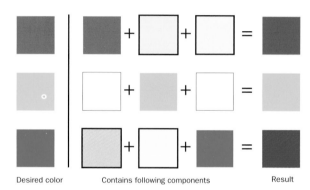

Desired color   Contains following components   Result

FIG 31 Separation filters and process inks are far from perfect. The various shortcomings add up to colors that are impure. The above illustration is exaggerated. The framed areas represent the undesirable elements that result in hue error, or contaminated colors.

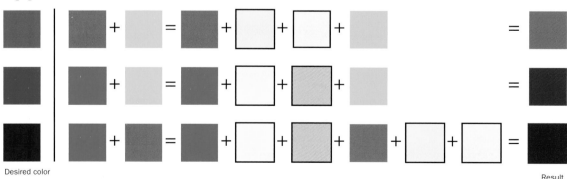

Desired color

Result

FIG 32 This is how the secondary colors are affected by deficiencies in separation filters and process inks. To the left are the desired colors. To the right are the resultant colors, and in between is shown how the colors are built up. The framed areas represent the undesirable color elements. Note that the illustration is highly exaggerated.

FIG 33 Three gray scales. The one to the left is built up of only the primary colors, and has a correct gray balance. The middle one is composed of only black, and can be used as a reference. The right one has too much magenta. It will produce a color tinge.

FIG 34 Example of how a typical skin tone, 60% Y, 40% M and 20% C (at left) is affected (at right) by the incorrect gray balance described in figure 33.

Neutral shades of gray are produced by mixing the three primary colors, cyan, magenta and yellow, in approximately equal proportions. Because of contaminant colors in the process inks, a certain amount of correction must be done to produce gray shades that are truly neutral. The gray balance is the amount of the three colors that must be used to create a neutral gray.

A correct gray balance necessary to produce good separations. If the gray balance is not correct, the entire image is affected—even those parts that are not gray. Shifts in hue occur in the image, and many of the colors look strange.

A balanced gray scale is created and printed in order to check the gray balance. As a comparison, a gray scale of black incorporating the same shade levels can be used.

In Adobe Photoshop, the gray balance can be adjusted under the *Printing Inks Setup* dialog box, by choosing the *Custom* setting for process ink definitions. A change in the gray balance can be seen if the neutral gray shades are read with the eyedropper, as well as on the curve in the *Separation Setup* dialog box. The gray balance normally does not need to be adjusted.

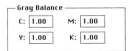

FIG 36 In Adobe Photoshop, the gray balance is often altered using these data. The value is initially 1.00 and this produces a good gray balance in most cases. If a value is reduced, the amount of that color decreases (its curve in figure 35 drops).

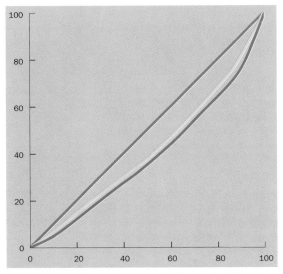

FIG 35 This is how a correct gray balance should look. Cyan is often used as a guideline for the desired gray value.

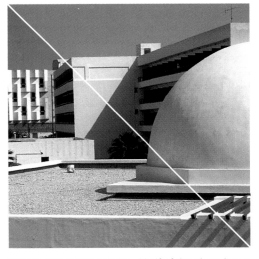

FIG 37 The upper right-hand half of the photo has a correct gray balance and the lower left-hand half has an incorrect gray balance.

A COLOR ORIGINAL often has a large tonal range: the difference between the lightest and the darkest tones. This is about 2.7 for a color slide, and about 2.0 for a paper print, as expressed in a logarithmic density scale. Such a wide tonal range is impossible to reproduce in printing, since colors cannot be printed on paper with the same high density as film tones. On very high-quality paper, used rarely, it is possible to reproduce a tonal range of about 1.9. Most printed matter has paper qualities that can withstand a tonal range of about 1.5. Newspaper has a range as low as 0.9, so during reproduction work, the tonal range must be compressed, the tones shaded closer to one another. Closely similar tones are merged into a single tone. For this reason, it is important to study the original, determine which areas are the most important, and note their tonal range. Then, the reproduction process can be optimized for these areas.

The tonal range of the printed image varies according to the quality of the paper and the density of the inks. Normally, efforts are made to restrict the tonal ranges of the printed image, in both the highlights and shadows. This is done so that the printed image does not look eroded in the diffuse highlight areas, and excessively thick in the darkest areas. The limits in figure 39 serve as a good recommendation. An exception must be made for small white surfaces that really are white—called specular highlights—and small surfaces that are to be totally black. The recommended limits apply to tonal values in the printed image. In the film, the tonal values must be somewhat less, in order to compensate for changes in tone (see page 46).

Another method for restricting tonal range is to set the limits so that all of the tonal values below a certain level (about 5%) are made white, and all the tonal values over a certain level (about 95%) are made black. This increases the image's contrast, and may work well in printing on newspaper. The best method must be found by trial and error, and a combination of the two can be used.

Approximate tonal ranges	
Paper print (b&w)	1.6
Paper print (color)	1.6
Color slide	2.7
Coated paper (high quality)	1.9
Coated paper (normal quality)	1.5
Newspaper	0.9

FIG 38 Above are some approximate tonal ranges for common originals and paper qualities.

Image type	Highlight	Shadow
Light	7%	97%
Midtone	5%	95%
Dark	3%	93%

FIG 39 This table shows the tonal limits for various image types. The data apply to the printed image in printing on newsprint, using web-fed offset.

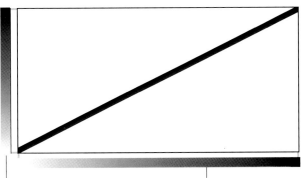

Tonal range after compression — Tonal range before compression

FIG 40 Tone compression takes place by compressing the original tonal range (the horizontal axis) down to the resultant tonal range (the vertical axis). When compression takes place along a straight line, it is called linear.

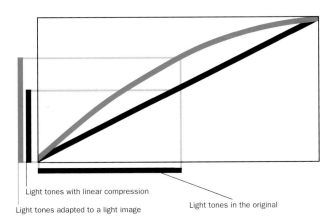

Light tones with linear compression

Light tones adapted to a light image

Light tones in the original

FIG 41 If tone compression does not take place along a straight line, it is nonlinear. If compression is to be adjusted for light images, the light tones are given greater tonal range than the dark. The gamma number for such a curve is less than 1.0.

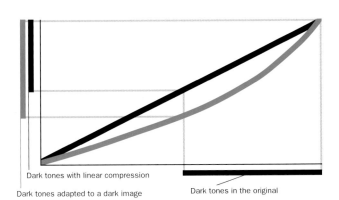

Dark tones with linear compression

Dark tones adapted to a dark image

Dark tones in the original

FIG 42 Here, tone compression has been adapted for a dark image. The dark tones in the original have been given a range of greater than half of the available tones. The gamma number for such a curve is higher than 1.0.

The first compression of tonal range takes place when scanning the original. At that time, the tonal curve can be adjusted to match the image type in question. This is normally done using a gamma value. Gamma values indicate the relationship between input and output data when a process step has been performed. Adjustments must be made later on in the process, as well. Adapting the reproduction process is vital to achieve high quality printing.

Factors that affect how the image should be handled are: what elements are important in the original; what it should convey; what type of paper it will be printed on; and how much the tonal values will change during output and offset printing. To get the best results, all of the links in the production chain must be known.

In order for results to be predictable and repeatable, the working process must be standardized and the equipment calibrated. The goal is for the same settings to produce the same result every time. Such a stable system is a prerequisite for reaching high quality.

The best gamma value for simulating the way we see tones is between 1.8 and 2.2. Therefore, 1.8 is a good gamma for scanning a normal midtone image and for adjusting your monitor. This redefines the 1.0 gamma used in figures 40 thru 42, to 1.8. This means that, for best tone reproduction, a light image should be scanned with a gamma under 1.8, and a dark image with a gamma greater than 1.8.

AN ORIGINAL IS converted into pixels using a scanner. There are scanners for various kinds of original artwork: slides, or paper prints. Some scanners work with both slides and paper prints.

Light is transmitted through a slide, or reflected off a paper print. This transmitted or reflected light passes through color filters that separate the red, green and blue wavelengths. The light then reaches CCD cells that sense the intensity of the light, and feed the data to the computer. CCD stands for Charge-Coupled Device, an array of photodiodes for converting light into digital data.

If the CCD cells work with 8 bits, the device sends out numerical values between 0 and 255 ($2^8=256$). This is done three times, once for each color filter. There are now CCD arrays on the market that sense the intensity of the three colors simultaneously, and do not require three filtered scans.

The number of CCD photodiodes per unit of length determines the scanner resolution. If there are 300 photodiodes per inch, the scanner has a resolution of 300 dpi (dots per inch).

The optical precision of the scanner determines how good the sharpness and color reproduction are. High optical precision means that a pixel-sized area of the original is registered on exactly one CCD photodiode. The result is excellent sharpness, and pure colors. Low precision means that adjacent photodiodes will partially register the same data, with poor sharpness and impure colors as the result.

The mechanical precision (registration) of a scanner must be good if each scan is to be exactly the same for each color. Poor mechanical precision may result in extra lines and color aberrations being added to the image.

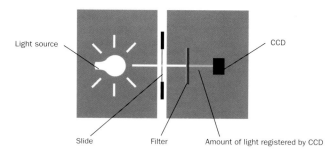
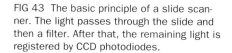

FIG 43 The basic principle of a slide scanner. The light passes through the slide and then a filter. After that, the remaining light is registered by CCD photodiodes.

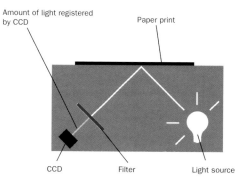

FIG 44 The basic principle of a scanner for paper prints. Light is reflected from the print and passes through a filter. Then, the remaining light is registered by the CCD photodiodes.

A computer works with 8 bits per pixel, per color. This means that each pixel is allocated one of the $2^8 = 256$ tones in each color: red, green and blue. This is called a 24-bit color depth, since $2^8 \cdot 2^8 \cdot 2^8 = 2^{24} = 16,777,216$ different color tones for each pixel.

If the CCD's photodiodes have a greater color depth than 8 bits, they will be able to differentiate more tones, which creates a greater dynamic range. Some scanners work with a 10-bit depth, or even more, which allows $2^{10} = 1024$ tones per color and pixel. The advantage here is that the choice of 256 tones to be used can be adapted according to the tone distribution of the original. A second advantage of scanning an original using more tones than necessary is that interference during scanning can be filtered out.

There are numerous manufacturers of scanners for DTP environments. An alternative to investing in a scanner is to use the Kodak Photo CD System. This system allows a conventional photo lab to handle the scanning, and then to supply the image stored on a Photo CD disk as well as on negatives and slides. In order to access the image on the CD, you will need a CD-ROM drive connected to your computer, as well as the necessary software.

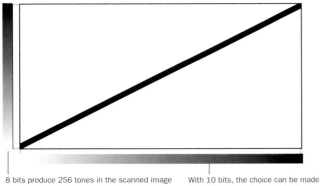

8 bits produce 256 tones in the scanned image | With 10 bits, the choice can be made from 1024 tones in the original.

FIG 45 If a scanner is able to read off more tones than can be stored in the computer, you can make a selection of tones can be made that is optimized for the tone distribution of the original.

FIG 46 This image was scanned in using the Kodak Photo CD System. It is supplied in compressed format on a CD disk. It is possible to open the image in one of five different resolutions, depending on what it will be used for. This image was opened in the second-highest resolution– 1,024 x 1,536 pixels.

T IS VERY IMPORTANT for subsequent image manipulation that the scanned image be as high-quality as possible. It is easy to correct a well-scanned image to make it even better, but it is almost impossible to enhance one that was poorly scanned.

As mentioned above, tone compression takes place during scanning. For this reason, the scanning parameters should be set so that the details in the more important areas of the original are picked up. This may mean that other, less important, details disappear. For example, giving priority to the shadow tones may cause the highlight tones to disappear.

It is the gamma value that controls which tonal areas in the image will be reproduced best. A dark original should be scanned with a higher gamma value than a light one. A high gamma value allows more of the available tones to reproduce dark areas (see also page 15).

To facilitate handling, it is useful to classify the original's tone distribution before scanning. Originals can be divided into three classes: snow images, midtone images, and night images. (Sometimes the terms "high-key," "medium," and "low-key" are also used.) This applies to both color and black and white.

Snow-image originals are characterized by about 70% to 90% of the image being taken up of light areas, in which the most important details are found. Light tones are also called diffuse highlight tones. The wholly white areas in the image are called specular highlights.

In midtone originals, the light and dark areas each take up about half of the image area, and the details are found in the midtone areas—tones between about 30% to 70% of white. Normally, there is an absence of details in the light and dark areas.

Night images consist mainly of dark tones, and the details are found in these dark areas. Dark tones are also known as shadow tones (or shadows).

FIG 47 This is a typical snow image. There are many diffuse details in the limestone walls of the light areas. In the dark areas of the image, the balconies and windows, there are no important details.

FIG 48 A typical night image is shown above. The clothes and details of the motorcycle are distinguishable in the dark areas. Details of the engine and helmet may be overexposed. The idea is to adjust the scanning parameters to bring out the dark areas as much as possible, without causing the engine and helmet details to disappear.

FIG 49 Above is a midtone photo with numerous details, and rather high contrast. The differences between light and dark tones are considerable.
Below is a midtone photo with low contrast and only a few fine details.

Classification, in other words, is not simply determining details in the lighter areas, but determining which areas of the original convey the main message.

Midtone originals are the easiest to reproduce. Snow images are also quite easy. The most important consideration with these originals is not to scan them so light that the details in the light areas disappear.

Night images are the most difficult. This is because most scanners on the market work with CCD technology. These devices have difficulty differentiating between similar tones in the dark areas. This type of original is also the hardest to reproduce on a printing press.

A good deal of time and effort should be directed toward learning to choose the right types of originals, knowing how to classify them, and to finding the correct scanning settings. These settings can typically be saved under distinctive names. When an original is scanned at some later time, you need only classify the image and then retrieve the proper file to set the scanner. This leads to greater simplification and efficiency.

Some types of originals may be difficult to scan with standard settings, but it is easiest to start with settings that are close, and modify them a little—for example, to compensate for color tinges.

It is always best to make adjustments as early in the production process as possible. This is why great care should be taken to get the best possible scan. That way, fewer corrections need to be made in the image-manipulation program.

IMAGES THAT ARE scanned into a computer can be stored in a number of formats. A format is a specific way to describe an image for computers, so that it can be saved on a hard disk or some other storage device. Below is an overview of the five most important formats, and what can be expected from them.

Photoshop format is Adobe Photoshop's default format for saving files if no other format is stipulated. (Cachet also uses this format.) A disadvantage is that Photoshop-format documents cannot be imported into page-layout programs. Images in RGB and CMYK modes can be saved in Photoshop-format.

TIFF-RGB format can be used to transfer images into other programs. Images in this format are not separated in CMYK mode. If they are to be printed with the colors separated, the importing program must be able to separate the colors. Advantages of the TIFF-RGB format are that it is relatively standardized, takes up little disk space, and is easy to compress, which saves even more disk space.

TIFF-CMYK format is nearly the same as TIFF-RGB, with the important difference that the images are separated in CMYK mode. This means that when importing images saved in TIFF-CMYK, all the separation settings, and compensation data, for tonal value changes have already been made. Transfer functions cannot be stored with images in TIFF-CMYK format. These images require about 1/3 more disk space than those in TIFF-RGB format.

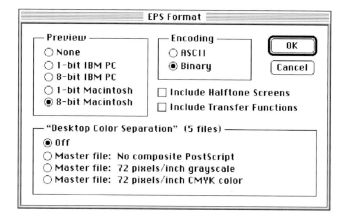

FIG 50 In Adobe Photoshop, separated images can be saved in TIFF-CMYK format or EPS format. For the EPS format, the *EPS Format* dialog box looks like this. There is a choice under *Preview* for the preview image to be in PICT (Macintosh) or TIFF (IBM PC) format, and displayed in black and white (1-bit) or color (8-bit). Under *Encoding,* there is a choice for the PostScript data to be either *ASCII* or *Binary*. Binary is the most common form. Whether halftone screen and transfer functions are to be stored with the image can also be chosen. The *"Desktop Color Separation" (5 files)* option furnishes DCS format files and under it, the color information for producing proofs on a color printer can be set.

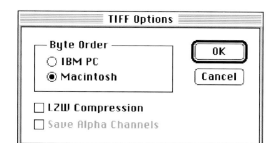

FIG 51 The TIFF format was designed to help transport images between IBM PC and Macintosh computers. The image can also be compressed using LZW compression. This nondestructive method causes the image to take up a little less space on the hard disk. For this compression method to be useful, the program in which the image will be used must be able to load compressed images. QuarkXPress can read LZW-compressed images, but it takes more time to load them than if they were not compressed.

Images in *EPS format* consist of PostScript data that define the image, and a low-quality preview (PICT for Macintosh and TIFF for IBM PC), which can be viewed on the monitor. Only the preview image is saved inside the document when the image is mounted on a page, so that the document will not take up unnecessary memory. There are links in the preview image that address PostScript data for output. If the resolution is low in the preview, the color reproduction is relatively good. If the image is saved in TIFF-CMYK format, the importing program must convert the color information back to RGB data, which can result in substantial color deviations.

DCS format is a type of EPS format in which the image is divided into five files—one file for each color, plus a preview image in low resolution that is linked to the color files. The advantage of this format is that the preview images take up little memory, and can easily be distributed on networks. During output, the color files are automatically addressed. PostScript data can also be saved in the preview image, which can be used to produce color proofs on a PostScript color printer.

Another advantage of both EPS and DCS formats is that the halftone screen settings (see page 5) and the transfer functions (see pages 46 and 73) can be saved with the image.

The file format can be chosen here.

If EPS is the chosen file format, normal EPS format or 5-file DCS format can be selected here.

It is possible to choose whether PostScript data in EPS and DCS formats should be in ASCII or binary codes. Binary coding takes up half as much memory, but not all programs and RIPs can access binary data.

You can choose whether the PICT image in EPS or DCS format will display in black and white or color. can be chosen.

Also in main file provides color information in PostScript language that can be used for producing proofs on a color printer.

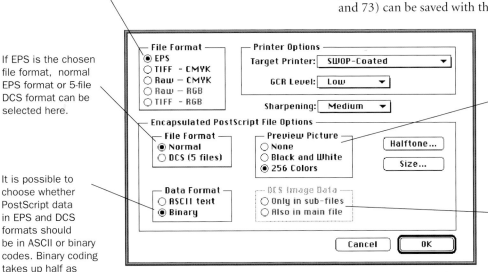

FIG 52 In Cachet, the separated images can be saved as EPS, DCS or TIFF-CMYK formats. Unseparated images can be saved in TIFF-RGB or PICT formats, or in Photoshop format.

THE PURPOSE OF a proof is to determine how the image will look in print. Proofs can be produced in several ways: by outputting to a color printer; by photographic/electrostatic methods, using separated films; or by printing on a press on regular paper. Printing on regular paper is expensive, but clearly the best, since it is done under the same conditions as will be used during production. This method of making proofs can prove to be economical, though, when producing expensive printed matter in long runs.

Proofs are also used as an important element in placing a printing job. The printing house should be able to duplicate the proof quality, and the customer should be able to use it as a legally binding sample, in case of future claims or complaints regarding printing quality.

Proofs that are not produced in a printing press are called prepress proofs. These are among the most common methods, and use lamination techniques. The four colors—cyan, magenta, yellow and black—are each applied, and each adhere, to a base that can simulate the final paper. The four bases are laminated together. This creates a laminated proof very close in quality to the final printed image, but the process is somewhat complicated and relatively expensive.

The fastest, least-expensive method is to output the image using a color printer. Color printers still have rather low resolution, which means that conventional halftone screening cannot be employed. It is also difficult to achieve a good match between a color printout and the final printed image. However, this problem can be solved by using a system like Apple ColorSync or EfiColor (see page 24).

Things to think about when using color-printer proofs

1. Does the printer use PostScript?

2. What paper sizes does the printer use?

3. Can the printer reproduce a bleed?

4. Is the printer memory sufficient?

5. Does the printer have enough color range able to simulate an offset printed image?

6. Is the printer fast enough?

7. What different kinds of paper can it use?

Bleed—when part of the print on a page (often the image) extends beyond the margin and to the edge of the paper.

In the case of laminated prepress proofs, a number of settings such as color reproduction, the various base types, tonal value changes and the different plastic coatings need to be carefully considered. The colors must agree with the color standard used (Eurostandard or SWOP), and should have the same density in the final printing.

There are a variety of bases available to simulate the different kinds of paper, and the resultant dot gains. The best solution is to use the same kind of paper as in the final printing. It may be possibile to add a final coating, to simulate glossy paper or the yellow tone found in newspaper.

When using color printers, you should check the paper size and color range, as well as the speed, output stability and amount of memory available. The paper size should be big enough to allow for bleeds. The color range should be broad enough to adequately simulate the colors of the standard you are using. Color files are often very large, so the output device must have sufficient memory and speed to manage the job.

In judging the proofs, it is important to know how they were produced, and what shortcomings the selected method might have. Usually, laminated proofs have a glossy surface that produces highly-saturated, distinct colors. When the image is later printed on newsprint, the output is not as good, and the customer is often disappointed. If the right method for pulling the proof had been used, or if the customer had been aware of the differences, misunderstandings could have been avoided.

Things to think about when using laminated proofs

1. Do the inks follow the color standard used (Eurostandard or SWOP)?

2. Is it possible to simulate the printing press's changes in tonal value?

3. Is the process complicated?

4. Can the process be carried out in daylight?

5. Can the final printing paper be used as a base?

6. What sizes are accepted by the equipment?

7. Does the equipment require a special environment, for example, due to poisonous chemicals?

FIG 53 The left photo has a bleed off the right margin, while the right photo has no bleed.

CALIBRATION is a process of adjusting the equipment in the production chain so that the settings can be recorded, and held constant during an extended period.

The devices that need to be calibrated are the scanner, the monitor, the imagesetter and the prepress printer. Of course, one must also calibrate the printing press, the equipment used to produce proofs, and even the printing plates—but this book covers only the links in the production cycle up to the output of film.

Many scanners calibrate themselves when they are turned on, or come with special calibration software. Calibration includes adjustment of the feeding mechanism for the original, or the CCD photodiodes, so that the color registration and sharpness are correct. The color balance is also adjusted, so that no color tinges are created during scanning.

The monitor is adjusted for satisfactory reproduction of tone, and for proper color balance. Tonal values are adjusted with the gamma value. A gamma number of 1.0 represents a linear reproduction of tone. The eye, however, perceives tones on a logarithmic scale, and the dark tones thus seem more compressed than the lighter ones. This can be simulated on the monitor by raising the gamma value.

Separation programs are calibrated so that the separation (the conversion from RGB to CMYK values) is carried out correctly, taking into consideration the adjustment of the monitor and the output device to be used, as well as other factors.

A supplement to Apple's system software, called ColorSync, has been developed to help keep track of the devices connected to the system, and to administer color conversions between them. Thus, color reproduction is kept the same, no matter what output device is used: a monitor, color printer or printing press. ColorSync works by maintaining profiles (special files of properties) for all the system devices.

original   display   print

FIG 54 In an uncalibrated system, the various units produce different results from the same original.

original   display   print

FIG 55 In a calibrated system, the various units produce the same results from the same original. If the system is absolutely calibrated, the units will produce results exactly the same as the original. This cannot, however, always be demanded, owing to the varying tone and color ranges of the units.

ColorSync uses the standardized CIE 1931 model (see page 11) as a color reference system. This means that all of the pixels are assigned coordinates in the CIE space, and that these coordinates are the same for the same original, no matter what scanner is used. When the image is displayed on the monitor screen, separated, or printed, each pixel is given a suitable RGB or CMYK value, adjusted for the profile of the device.

FIG 56 This photo has no extra compensation for contaminated colors.

FIG 57 This photo has been given extra compensation for contaminated colors, according to the method described below.

These profiles describe the color properties of each unit when calibrated. With their help, ColorSync determines how the conversion should be carried out. If Apple's model for color conversion is unsatisfactory, ColorSync can be supplemented with models from independent manufacturers. There are a number of such models on the market. One is EfiColor, developed by Electronics for Imaging, Inc. EfiColor is used by Cachet, and some other programs. Another model for color conversion is Color-Sense from Kodak.

In Adobe Photoshop, the printing inks' CIE definitions can be altered, which affects how the RGB values are converted into CMYK values.

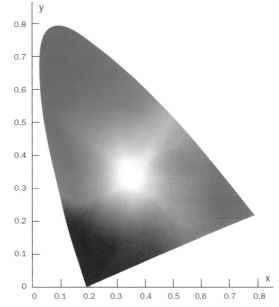

FIG 59 This is a chromaticity diagram of a CIE system encompassing all colors seen by the eye. This diagram actually cannot be printed, since the printable colors are considerably fewer in number (see page 11).

FIG 58 Assume that you want to compensate for an undesirable element of yellow in magenta, resulting in an orangish red. The values for red (MY) are x=0.5760 and y=0.3349. The red in the photo appears orange-red, so that must be expressed in CIE values. This corresponds to the red hues being closer to the yellow area in the chromaticity diagram. Choose *Custom* and enter y=0.37 instead. You will then see that the red color field becomes more orange. Contaminated colors in the other colors can be compensated for in a similar way.

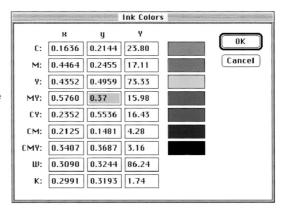

	x	y	Y	
C:	0.1636	0.2144	23.80	
M:	0.4464	0.2455	17.11	
Y:	0.4352	0.4959	73.33	
MY:	0.5760	0.37	15.98	
CY:	0.2352	0.5536	16.43	
CM:	0.2125	0.1481	4.28	
CMY:	0.3407	0.3687	3.16	
W:	0.3090	0.3244	86.24	
K:	0.2991	0.3193	1.74	

I N SCANNING, a number of parameters should be considered: whether scanning is to be in black and white or color; the resolution that will be used; the area to be scanned; and the tone distribution of the original image.

The scanner is controlled either by an independent software package, or through a plug-in module to another program. With a plug-in module, you can access the image directly from inside an image-manipulation or page-layout program. In most of the control programs for scanners, a low-resolution image is first scanned and displayed on the monitor. You can then indicate what part of the original is of interest, and scan only that part of the image. Images take up a great deal of space on hard disks, which is why it is unwise to store parts of an image that will not be needed.

Next, the scanning resolution should be adjusted for the size and screen frequency of the printed image. Excessive resolution only takes up unnecessary disk space without any improvement in quality. How to calculate the required resolution is explained in the section RESOLUTION on page 8.

The most difficult step in the scanning procedure is adapting the settings to the tone distribution of the original. After having classifying the original (see ORIGINAL TYPES on page 18), you need to choose a suitable tone curve.

A night image should be scanned with a high gamma value, and a snow image with a low one. A midtone image should have a gamma value near 1.0.

The goal of scanning, and of the subsequent processing, is to produce an image on the monitor that is as close to the desired printed result as possible. Then, settings need to be chosen to make this possible. In other words, it is wrong to scan in an image on the light side, in order to compensate for later dot gain. Instead, the original would be scanned so that the image on the monitor looks like it will when printed on paper. Then, you should correct for dot gain by other means.

FIG 60 This column of images is the way the photos should look when the correct scanning parameters are used.

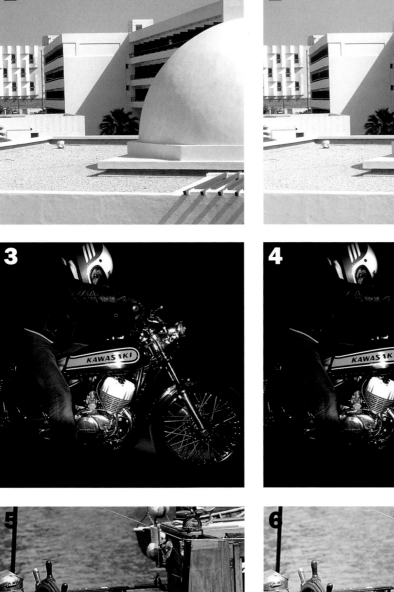

FIG 61 Here you can see how important it is to use the right parameters during scanning. Photos 1 and 3 were scanned as midtone images; photos 2 and 6, as night images; and photos 4 and 5, as snow images. Subsequent attempts to correct for these errors will inevitably produce poorer results than if the correct settings had been used from the start.

CORRECTING THE TONE distribution of an original may be necessary if the scanning settings were not correct, or if the image's appearance is to be modified (the midtones or shadows made lighter).

The factors governing the tone distribution of an image are lightness and contrast, as well as black-and-white point settings, and the settings for highlight, midtone and shadow values. To describe an image's tone distribution, a histogram is used. The height of each bar indicates the number of pixels of a specific tonal value, and its location on the axis shows the tonal value referred to.

One way to show changes in tone distribution is to draw a curve with the original tonal values (before adjustment) on the y-axis, and the new tonal values on the x-axis. If this curve sags downward, the gamma value is high. If it is a straight line, the gamma value is 1.0. A curve that bulges upward represents a low gamma value. The tonal values begin with white, and become darker to the right and upward in the diagram.

In order to restrict the tonal values in the brightest and darkest parts of the image (see page 14), the end points of the curve should be raised or lowered. It is a good idea to save such curves, so that they can be used when changing tone distribution. Note that the contrast is reduced somewhat when restrictions of this kind are introduced. This may make the image look a little washed-out, but most of the time the appearance is improved. Try the various settings and observe what happens, before deciding whether to carry out such changes.

Tone-distribution limits can also be introduced with transfer functions, but since transfer functions do not affect the image on the monitor, the printed result will diverge from the screen image. On the other hand, the restrictions take place more automatically when using transfer functions than when using curves.

FIG 62 A histogram showing the tone distribution of an image. The dark tones are to the left, and the light tones to the right. The height of each bar indicates how many pixels have a certain tonal value (how great an area of the image has a certain tonal value).

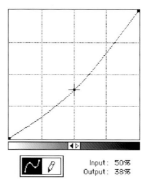

Input: 50%
Output: 38%

FIG 63 A tonal value diagram is used to show how the tonal values of the image have been altered. The original tonal values are on the x-axis; the new tonal values are on the y-axis. In this case, all the pixels having tonal values of 50% are altered to 38%. The other tones in the image change according to the curve.

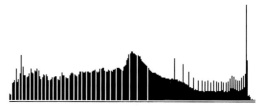

FIG 64 Since the image has been made lighter, the tones have been displaced toward the lighter areas. The white strips and black spikes occur because there are only 256 halftones, and these have been redistributed (compressed) into a smaller area.

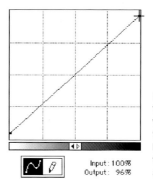

Input: 100%
Output: 96%

FIG 65 This is the way a tonal value diagram looks when the limits of 4% and 96%, respectively, have been introduced for halftone values. The result is a reduction in contrast.

FIG 66 An image direct from a scanner.

FIG 67 The image has been made lighter in accordance with figure 63.

FIG 68 The tonal values have been restricted, in accordance with figure 65.

Once an image has been scanned, it must be color-corrected to compensate for any shortcomings of the output device at the end of the production cycle. This should be done automatically as much as possible, but a certain amount of manual correction may be necessary. Corrections are mainly done to make the final printed image look like the original.

Automatic correction is carried out somewhat differently in each separation program. Generally, it compensates for contaminated colors in the process inks and separation filters. Automatic color correction is done during conversion from the RGB mode to the CMYK mode. For further details see CALIBRATION on page 24.

Manual correction can be applied to the entire image, or selectively to certain colors or areas. The goal of manual correction is to reinforce the effects of automatic correction, or to alter colors in the image with respect to the original. This correction can be carried out in two modes: RGB mode or CMYK mode. RGB mode is the best one to work in.

The advantage of working in RGB mode is that changes in the image can be made before deciding how much black must be generated. In this way, no commitment need be made initially for a certain amount of black generation, and the image remains sensitive to color changes. A disadvantage is that the similarity of the monitor image to the final printed image is poorer than in the CMYK mode. On the other hand, programs offer measuring tools that can be used to view CMYK values prior to separation.

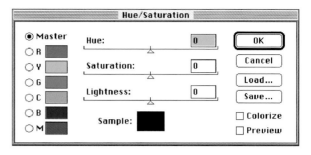

FIG 69 The *Hue/Saturation* dialog box in Adobe Photoshop is based on the color wheel principle. The *Hue* slider control changes the hue: it moves the colors around the circle. The *Saturation* slider control increases saturation, drawing the colors toward the periphery.

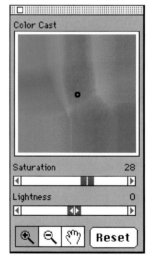

FIG 70 In Cachet, colors are generally corrected throughout the entire image with the *Color* palette. It has a color surface that can be used to change hues, and slider controls for regulating saturation and lightness.

FIG 71 A color wheel looks like this—cyan is located 60 degrees counter-clockwise from green, and yellow is 60 degrees clockwise. Directly across from green is magenta. When the hue is altered, the colors move around the circle, and when saturation is altered, the colors are drawn out toward the periphery, where the colors are fully saturated.

FIG 72 This is the way a photo looks with no color correction. The colors appear dull and impure.

FIG 73 Here, saturation has been intensified throughout the entire photo. But the colors of the lettuce, radishes and salmon still look dull. Selective color correction is needed.

Selective color correction also varies from program to program. In Adobe Photoshop, six primary colors are chosen, and they then affect all of the colors in the image that contain those primaries as a dominant component. In Cachet, the image colors to be altered are chosen by clicking on them using a special tool. In both programs, parts of the image that will not be modified can be masked. If a red hue is altered in one part of the image, another red hue in another part of the image need not be affected.

It is a good idea to save the selected color corrections for later use with another image. A library can be built up in this way, containing various settings to fit different types of images.

You may often want to make the colors in an image cleaner. This is done by reducing, or wholly eliminating, the color's third component. A red color, for instance, will become redder if it is completely stripped of cyan, and a green will become greener without any magenta. When achromatic reproduction is used (see SEPARATION, page 35), it is the black component that causes contaminant color. It is advisable to have a measuring instrument handy when performing selective color correction. In Adobe Photoshop, the *Color Palette* is used, and in Cachet, the *Color Meter*.

Remember that the monitor in most cases can display more saturated colors than can be printed. In Adobe Photoshop, it is possible to check if the colors are printable using the *Color Picker* dialog box. In Cachet, there is a special tool called *Gamut Alarm*. The programs automatically adjust the colors to the printable color range, but to see how that will look, the image displayed on the monitor must be manually adjusted. This can be difficult, and often results in poorer results than with automatic adaptation.

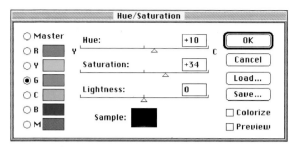

FIG 74 In Adobe Photoshop, selective color correction can be done using the *Hues/Saturation* dialog box. If the lettuce in the photo is to be made greener, *G* is set as the dominant color and its saturation level is increased—magenta is removed. The balance between yellow and cyan is adjusted using the *Hue* slider control. To lighten the colors, the *Brightness* slider control is used. To modify only the lettuce, and not the woods or the other green areas of the photo, the selection tools are used to create a mask before choosing the *Hue/Saturation* dialog box. Then, only the selected area will be affected.

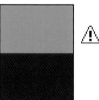

FIG 75 In Cachet, the *Gamut Alarm* dialog box shows which image colors cannot be reproduced correctly by the output device. In Adobe Photoshop, a warning triangle appears in the *Color Picker* dialog box for those colors that cannot be reproduced.

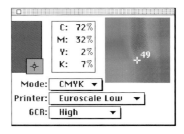

FIG 76 In Cachet, one or more colors are selected for correction with the magic wand tool. Masking is done with a rectangular or elliptical tool, or with the lasso tool. Only the colors inside the mask will be affected by palette changes. The palette has the same controls as the palette for general color correction, and works the same way. To see color values, use the *Color Meter* tool, which displays values for the colors according to the profile chosen.

FIG 77 Selective color correction has been carried out for the lettuce, radishes, salmon, wood, and table cloth. Corrections must be made for each color, which can be rather time-consuming.

N THEORY, a color image can be built up of the three primary process inks: cyan, magenta and yellow. But owing to imperfections in the colorants, black must be used to reinforce the contrast.

There are three main methods to generate the black areas in separations: Skeleton Black, Under Color Removal, and Gray Component Replacement, or GCR. GCR is also called achromatic reproduction.

With skeleton black, only the darkest tones of the image, where black is added on top of the three primary colors, will have an effect. A disadvantage in using this method is that up to four full-color layers can be found in the dark areas of an image. Together, that makes 400% color (100% for each color). This causes technical problems with ink trapping and drying in printing. (Ink trapping is the ability of one ink layer to accept another.)

These problems are greatest in the dark areas of an image. For this reason, some of the colors are replaced with black. This method is called Under Color Removal, or UCR, and it works only in the neutral tones—that is, those that are composed of equal parts of the primary colors.

Another disadvantage of building up neutral gray shades using primary colors is that the image becomes sensitive to gray-balance deviations. Registration errors during printing can also easily produce undesirable color tinges.

Black replacement can be taken so far that it affects all of the tertiary colors (see page 10), so that there are never more than two primary colors plus black, at any point in the image. This method is called achromatic repro and has the advantage of radically reducing the total amount of color. Gray balance becomes almost perfect using achromatic repro, since the neutral gray shades are built up of black only. Furthermore, the chance of getting color tinges due to off-registration is reduced, since a maximum of only three colors are printed on top of each other.

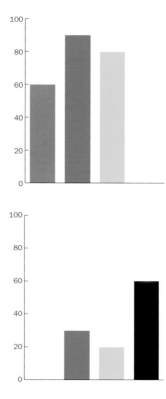

FIG 78 Without achromatic repro, a brown color like this, completely lacking black, builds up.

FIG 79 Achromatic repro works like this: Equal portions of the primary colors are removed, so that one of them disappears. The share of the removed color is replaced with black. Owing to imperfections in the processing inks, however, the actual replacement is done as in figure 81.

FIG 80 A brown color consisting of:

60% cyan
90% magenta
80% yellow
0% black
_____
230% in total

FIG 81 The same color achromatically:

0% cyan
77% magenta
47% yellow
62% black
_____
186% in total

FIG 82 Black **without** Under Color Addition:

0% cyan
0% magenta
0% yellow
100% black

FIG 83 Black **with** 45% Under Color Addition:

47% cyan
33% magenta
33% yellow
100% black

FIG 84 This photo has been separated with the setting *GCR Heavy* in Adobe Photoshop, since it contains so much gray. This corresponds to achromatic repro. The image takes up 18 Mb of disk space when separated. The half-tone screen frequency is 150 lpi, and the sampling factor is 1.8.

Full achromatic repro need not be used. But even partial application will still affect all tertiary colors. This differs from UCR, which affects only the neutral tones.

Achromatic repro is preferred for web-fed offset printing of newspapers, in which drying time and correct registration are critical factors. This method is the most frequently used for all kinds of repro work, but its desirability varies according to the conditions. One disadvantage of the method is that sensitive color transitions in the light areas, such as skin tones, can become too sharp.

Black tones that are printed solely with black are always difficult to reproduce with high saturation; they instead appear grayish. This is because black process ink lacks ample density. This is solved by adding a certain amount of primary colors beneath the black layer, a process called *Under Color Addition* (UCA). This method is normally used not for images, but for large black color plates (see figure 83).

The generation of black separations also depends on the separation program used. In some programs, you can choose the achromatic degree, or GCR, to be used. In other programs, it is possible to designate curves and other parameters governing how black generation is to be carried out. A few examples of the various separation methods, using Adobe Photoshop, are shown here.

An important detail to remember is that conversion from RGB mode to CMYK mode is not wholly reversible: the image will take on somewhat different colors if returned to RGB mode after having been switched to CMYK mode. The reason for this is that the number of reproducible colors differs for the two modes. To go back to the RGB mode, the image must be closed without saving and the old image re-opened. Or, of course, the *Revert* command can be used.

SEPARATION

CMY K

FIG 85 Separated using *UCR* in Adobe Photoshop.

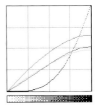

FIG 86 Separated using the *Light GCR* option in Adobe Photoshop.

FIG 87 Separated using the *Medium GCR* option in Adobe Photoshop.

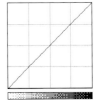

FIG 88 Separated using the *Maximum GCR* option in Adobe Photoshop.

A DOBE PHOTOSHOP HAS a number of functions, tools, and filters for manipulating images—everything from simple retouching of damaged film, to complete changes in the appearance of a photograph.

This spread and the next show a number of examples of how images can be manipulated. The possibilities are practically limitless. Images can be altered, several images can be merged, parts of images can be placed in other images, colors can be manipulated, and color photos can be turned into black and white. Most of the functions can work with all or part of an image.

On pages 42 and 43 are some examples of images that were created partially or wholly with Adobe Photoshop. One of them has a photograph as the original, and the other three were drawn on a computer.

A color image scanned from a slide is used as a starting point.

The color image is converted into a gray-scale image by changing the mode in the *Mode* menu.

The *Emboss* filter was used on a gray-scale image to create a relief effect.

The *Threshold* command was used to convert the gray shades of the image into only black and white.

The original image before processing.

Find Contour filter was applied.

Lens flare filter was used.

Spherize filter produces effects similar to a wide-angle lens with a very short focal length.

Watercolor filter from Aldus Gallery Effects.

Pointillize filters the image into irregular points.

This is the way the original looks. It has not undergone any image manipulation, except what is necessary to achieve high printing quality: some tone and color correction, and application of the filter *Unsharp Mask*.

Here, quite a bit of retouching has been carried out. The shore in the background has been replaced by the horizon and a lighthouse, the surfboard on the pier and the fork near the radishes have been removed, potatoes have been put on the plate to the far right, small dust particles on the original slide have been removed, and the sailboat has been vertically straightened. With all the possibilities presented by electronic image manipulation, it is important to understand that photos no longer have their traditional intrinsic value as evidence.

Image Manipulation:
Anders Blomberg/ElectroPix

The photo has now been processed twice, using the filter *Facet*. Compare this to the original on page 40. The border has been given a feathered edge, by selecting it and using the *Feather* command. After that, the selection has been reversed and then deleted, using the Backspace key.

Here, the photo has been modified using the *Add Noise* command, to achieve a grainy effect. It has been diffused toward white using the *Feather* command.

Here, a graphic illustration from Adobe Illustrator has been combined with a scanned image in Adobe Photoshop. The transparency of the inserted illustration has been varied, and the image itself modified using the *Curves* command .

Image manipulation:
Anders F. Rönnblom
Studio Matchbox

This illustration was originally drawn in Adobe Illustrator as a very simple object. The image was then imported into Fractal Painter and Adobe Photoshop, for additional manipulation and color separation. To the right is the original from Adobe Illustrator. It was automatically separated by QuarkXPress during printout.

Illustration: *Anders Blomberg/ElectroPix*

A family "picture" composed by Anders Blomberg in Adobe Photoshop and Fractal Painter. The black border around it was created in QuarkXPress. It was given extra saturation by *Under Color Addition* of approximately 40% cyan, magenta and yellow under the black.

THE DUPLEX HALFTONES method is used to reproduce monochrome images with an enhanced number of halftones. Printing black ink on white paper can produce about 50 to 60 tones. To increase the number of tones, and thereby give the image greater depth, it is printed twice, using different screen angles and tone distribution.

The first printing is in black. It reproduces the dark areas of the original. The second printing can also be in black, but often a dark gray ink is chosen. It reproduces the light areas of the original.

If instead, primary colors are chosen for the second printing, the method is called duotone. Duotone is a simple, inexpensive way to improve originals and make the printed matter more attractive without using four colors.

Duplex images can be created in Adobe Photoshop by converting a gray-scale image. This is done using the Duotone command in the Mode menu.

The colors to be used, and their particular tone distributions, are set in the dialog box displayed when this command is chosen.

Colors are selected by clicking on the desired color in the Color Picker, by specifying the color's composition, or by selecting a PMS color. Screen angle and frequency is determined the same way as for four-color images.

PMS stands for Pantone Matching System and is a range of standardized colors often used as references in printing.

In the duplex mode, it is also possible to create multi-tone images using three or four colors. The third or fourth color is specified in the same way as the others.

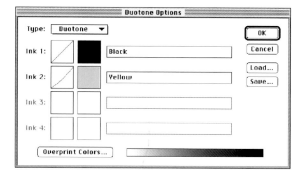

FIG 89 This is the way the dialog box might look for a duplex image to be printed in black and yellow. The black is lightened somewhat and the other color (yellow in this case) is made a little thinner. A number of suitable curves are supplied with Adobe Photoshop for Duotone, Tritone and Quadtone (four colors).

The colors must be given names that can be found in the color menu of the QuarkXPress document in which the image is to be mounted. If the color is not found in the QuarkXPress menu, it will be necessary to create a color with the correct name. Although it need not look like the color in Adobe Photoshop, it is easier to keep track of if it does.

Remember that a duplex image in Adobe Photoshop does not consist of two layers. Instead, an image is created for each color from the original gray-scale image, according to the curves set in the dialog box. The colors cannot be modified separately only the entire resulting image.

1. The original black and white photo.
2. Four-color separated photo. Printed in cyan, magenta, yellow and black, in order to increase the number of tones and thusthe depth of the image.
3. Black and cyan give a "cold" impression.
4. Black and yellow give a "warm" impression.

1

2

3

4

CHANGES IN TONAL values take place in several stages of the reproduction process. Tones in an image tend to become darker, especially in the printing stage. To compensate for these changes, the image tones must be lightened. Tonal changes may vary widely, depending on the printing process and the paper to be used. For web-fed offset, values may shift as much as 30% to 40%, whereas for sheet-fed offset using coated paper, it may be 10% to 20% for the same tonal areas. Various factors affect tonal values, particularly the mechanical dot gain that occurs during printing. As a guide, here is a review of the most common reasons for tonal value changes.

Tonal values may change slightly when the films are produced by the imagesetter. The reason for this is that an imagesetter commonly uses excess black. Usually, this can largely be eliminated with the help of a calibration program. It is often assumed that this change in tonal value is negligible (about 1–2%), but it should be checked regularly.

Another source of tonal value changes may be the contact copying of the film and printing plates. Therefore, one should avoid making too many contact copies of the film. The finished film should be taken straight from the imagesetter.

Dot loss occurs when plates are copied from positive film; copying from negative film causes dot gain. Dot loss can be an advantage, since it partly compensates for the dot gain that will occur during printing.

Tonal values can also shift because of an enlargement of the printed color dots, which may be caused by an incorrect chemical balance between ink and moisture.

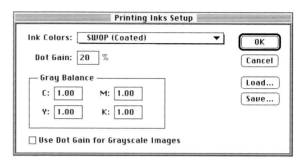

FIG 90 Adobe Photoshop has a *Dot Gain* command in the *Printing Inks Setup* dialog box. This compensates for a change in tonal value for the 50% tonal range, according to what is specified in the dialog box, and for the rest of the tonal range according to a curve similar to the one in figure 97. Compensation of this kind affects how the image should be converted from RGB mode to CMYK mode.

The *Compress CMYK gamut into RGB gamut* box ensures that the entire CMYK space is used, and is not restricted by what may be displayed on the monitor. The result is better colors in the image.

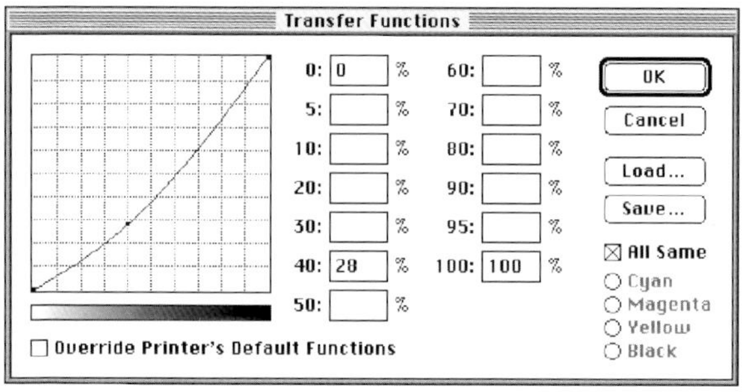

FIG 91 Another alternative is to compensate using transfer functions. This is done by saving a transfer function with each image. The transfer function does not affect how the image is separated from RGB mode to CMYK mode. Compensation is performed when the separations are transferred to the RIP for output. The transfer function is found in the *Transfer Function* dialog box, which is displayed when the *Transfer* button is clicked in the *Page Setup* dialog box.

Transfer functions can only be saved with images in EPS and DCS formats.

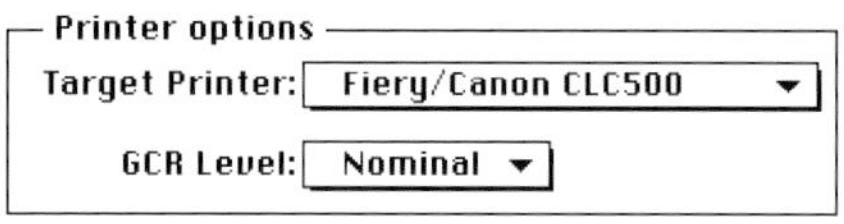

FIG 92 In Cachet, which uses EfiColor technology, color compensation is included in the profile. One need only keep the tonal value changes within the limitations specified in the profile.

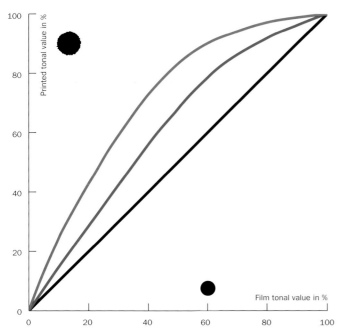

FIG 93 The tonal values of a printed image, relative to the tonal values of the films: the red curve applies to web-offset printing on newspaper and the green, to sheet-fed printing on coated paper. The curves will vary slightly according to according to the printing press used, but their magnitude and form should be approximately as shown.

As mentioned before, mechanical dot gain is a more common type of tonal value change than chemical or optical changes. Mechanical dot gain occurs when process inks are absorbed by the paper into an area larger than the corresponding screen dot. It is dependent on the ink-feed control and other printing press settings, and the surface smoothness of the paper.

Optical dot gain does not actually change the size of the dot, but makes it look larger. This is due to light being reflected from the underlying paper, despite the ink on top. Optical dot gain becomes more noticeable as the roughness of the paper increases.

The three types of tonal-value changes frequently interact to bring about considerable dot gain. Some of this can be eliminated by adjusting printing press settings, but one must compensate for the rest in the repro process.

Dot gain may also vary from one process ink to another, and from one screen frequency to another. For this reason, dot gain should always be checked ahead of time in any press to be used for producing big, expensive runs.

Changes in tonal value can be compensated for in a number of ways. The goal is to make the screened images lighter, so that they end up with the desired tonal values.

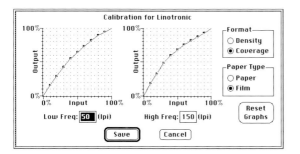

FIG 94 In order to carry out compensation according to the stipulated curves, the *Calibrated output* box in the *Print* dialog box must be checked. Compensation is performed only on images saved in TIFF format, images saved in EPS format in Adobe Illustrator, or screens created in QuarkXPress. Images saved in EPS format and DCS format from Adobe Photoshop and Cachet, with or without transfer functions, are not affected. If transfer functions are used, color compensation will be governed by those functions.

FIG 95 An additional compensation method for tonal value changes is to use the Calibration XTension to QuarkXPress. In this case, compensation is first performed during output. The images need not have any other compensation performed by using the *Dot Gain* command.

FIG 96 When *Calibration* is used, the tonal values are fed into a gray scale, and *Calibration* then computes the proper compensation. Tonal values for two different screen frequencies are entered. If another frequency is used, however, then *Calibration* will compute the proper compensation with the help of the values from the stated curves. Since different curves are to be stipulated for paper and film, the right material must be chosen in *Page Setup* if the correct curve is to be used.

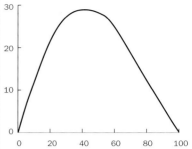

FIG 97 Here, dot gain has been drawn as a curve. The y-axis shows dot gain in absolute percentage, and the x-axis shows the tonal value of the film. The maximum dot gain is 30% in the 50% tone. That means that 50% on film will be 80% in print.

FIG 98 This is how the film looks with a compensation for tonal value change of 30%. The color layers look similar, and tonal values in the *Color* and *Info* palettes show these values. Of course, the imagesetter must be correctly calibrated.

FIG 99 This is the way the photo should look if printed correctly without changes in tonal value. The measured values in the *Color* palette and *Info* palette will match these tonal values.

FIG 100 This is the way the image is displayed on the monitor, and the way it looks in print with a tonal value change of 30%.

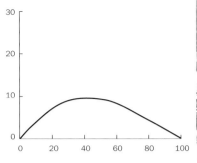

FIG 101 Here, the maximum dot gain is 10% in the 50% tone. This means that 50% on the film will only be 60% in print. The dynamic tonal range of the photo will then increase, compared to figure 97.

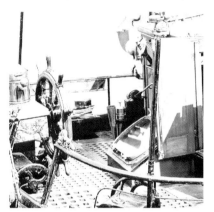

FIG 102 This is the way the films look with a compensation for tonal value change of 10%. They are substantially darker than the corresponding films adjusted for 30% tonal value change (figure 98).

FIG 103 This ideal image is only minutely lighter than the original photo.

FIG 104 This photo is the same as in figure 100, both on the monitor and in print. If the monitor is in RGB mode, the image's appearance on screen will not change when the compensation for dot gain is altered. If displayed in CMYK mode, it is already separated with a certain amount of compensation, and its appearance on screen will change if a different dot gain is stipulated. The tonal values of the film will not change, however. This way, it is possible to simulate how altered dot gain in the printing process will affect the appearance of the images.

THE SHARPENING FILTER is used to electronically enhance the "focus" of an image. The most common, and best, way to sharpen an image is to use the Unsharp Mask filter. This filter works by converting the image into a matrix of square pixels, then adding an outline. The area under the outline in the original image is made somewhat blurred, by reducing the contrast between adjacent pixels. The image's size determines how wide the radius of this blurred area should be.

The edge of the synthetic outline is made somewhat darker than the original, and then copied into the original image. The blurred outline unites with the copied sharp edge to produce an image that appears sharper.

Keep the texture of the image in mind when setting the value of the Unsharp Mask. Images with soft tonal transitions should be sharpened less, while those with many small details may require more processing.

In Adobe Photoshop, the monitor provides a good idea of the quality of an image's sharpness when the scale 1:2 is used. Images that are to be printed using a coarse screen will turn out better if they look a bit "too sharp" on the monitor.

FIG 105 This is the way a greatly magnified gray element looks. The peripheral edge is blurred. The contrast between adjacent pixels is low.

FIG 106 After using the Unsharp Mask filter, the element looks like this. A pronounced black edge is seen. The element has been made a little blurred immediately outside and inside the blackened edge.

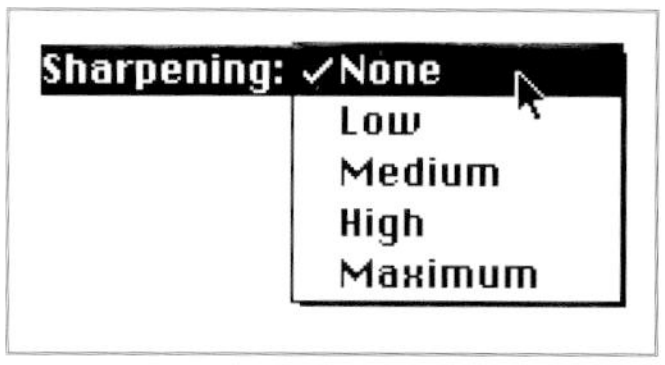

FIG 107 In Cachet, one first sets the level of sharpening, and the program then determines the radius based on the number of pixels forming the image. The threshold value is adjusted so that small stray particles are not amplified.

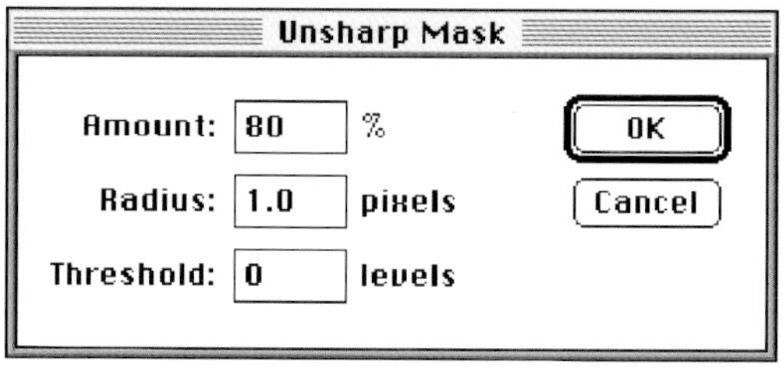

FIG 108 This is the way the Unsharp Mask dialog box in Adobe Photoshop looks. It is used to set Amount, Radius and Threshold. The *Amount* specifies how much darker the edge of the outline image should be. The *Radius* specifies the width of the outline. The *Threshold* value is used to avoid amplifying stray particles or scratches on the original. The value may be between 0 and 225. A low value results in high sensitivity. Normally, a value of zero is used.

FIG 109 This is the way a photo looked before using the Unsharp Mask filter.

FIG 110 Unsharp Mask filter has been used in Adobe Photoshop. The parameters were *Amount* 120%, *Radius* 1 pixel and *Threshold* 0.

FIG 111 This is the way the photo turns out if Unsharp Mask filtering is exaggerated. The three parameters were 400%, 1 pixel and 0.

COLOR IMAGES OFTEN take up vast amounts of hard disk space. Storing them thus requires high-capacity hard disks. Sending such images via modem can also be time-consuming.

To reduce the size of image files for long-term storage (for example, in an archive), as well as for transmission over telephone lines, various ways of compressing images have been developed. There are now two main groups: destructive and non-destructive compression. The latter does not alter the quality of the image, but can only compress it down to about half the size of the original file.

Destructive image compression removes information from the image, though in a way that affects the quality of the image as little as possible. One way to compress an image is to use the so-called JPEG algorithm. JPEG, which stands for Joint Photographic Expert Group, was developed to become the standard image compression method. A number of products on the market use this algorithm. On the facing page are some examples of images compressed in JPEG.

Compression should be done only after color correction and other image manipulation. The image must be expanded before it can be separated, and separated images can at present, only be compressed non-destructively.

The appropriate degree of compression depends on what the image is to be used for. If it is to be coarsely screened and printed on low-quality paper, a higher degree of compression can be used than if fine screening and high-quality paper are involved.

Different images are affected differently by compression. You should therefore always test to find the right degree of compression for the image type and reproduction conditions you are using.

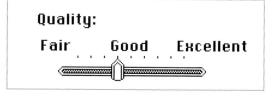

FIG 112 Plug-in programs for Adobe Photoshop and Cachet let you specify the desired image quality level before compressing. The lower the quality, the greater the degree of compression.

FIG 113 This is a photo that has not been compressed at all. It takes up 3,299 Kb of disk space.

FIG 114 Here, the photo is shown after being compressed, with the slider control set on medium quality. Then it takes up 761 Kb.

FIG 115 This photo was compressed with the slider control set on low quality; it now takes up 86 Kb.

T IS IMPORTANT to maintain correct alignment, or registration, between the four separated films when their images are transferred to paper.

Even if correct registration is carefully maintained, a small amount of misalignment almost always takes place between the printed colors. This is caused by the stretching and shrinking of the paper in both length and width, as it is fed through the printing press. This misregistration varies from one printing process to another. Web-fed offset, the process used most often for daily newspapers, is the most sensitive. If the misregistration is sufficiently small, the average eye will hardly notice it; but if it is excessive, it may seriously degrade the sharpness and details of the printed image.

Tinted panels, colored lines and letters are very sensitive to misregistration. This is particularly true against a colored background. Misregistration will result in irritating white gaps where the white paper shows through between the colors.

To reduce the risk of these gaps, a technique called trapping was developed. Trapping works by creating an overlap zone, or stroke, so that the process inks will slightly overprint. This stroke is diminished to bridge any gap caused by misregistration. This technique is not used for halftone images, since the colors and tonal values would be affected.

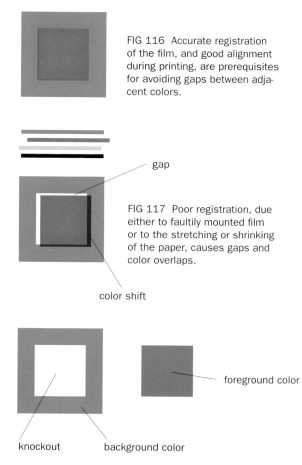

FIG 116 Accurate registration of the film, and good alignment during printing, are prerequisites for avoiding gaps between adjacent colors.

gap

FIG 117 Poor registration, due either to faultily mounted film or to the stretching or shrinking of the paper, causes gaps and color overlaps.

color shift

foreground color

knockout   background color

FIG 118 Key terms used in trapping technique.

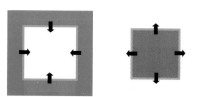

FIG 119 Traditional trapping works by "spreading" the foreground color, or "choking" the background color, when separation films are made. The light outline in the figure shows spreading and choking, respectively.

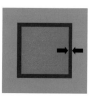

FIG 120 If desktop trapping is used, a line, or "stroke," is created around the foreground color. The width of this stroke determines the magnitude of the misregistration before a gap will appear. Dark text should not be spread against a light background, since it will alter the shape of the letters.

FIG 121 In QuarkXPress, in the *Preferences* sub-menu under the *Edit* menu, there is a command called *Application* that displays the dialog box shown below. The box is used to set how automatic trapping is to be carried out.

```
┌─Trap──────────────────────────────┐
│ Auto Method:    [ Absolute ]      │
│ Auto Amount:    [ 0,144  pt ]     │
│ Indeterminate:  [ 0  pt ]         │
│ Overprint Limit: [ 95% ]          │
│ ⊠ Ignore White    ⊠ Process Trap  │
└───────────────────────────────────┘
```

Ignore White inhibits spreading of the foreground color over white areas.

Checking the *Process Trap* box will cause spreading **after** separation, with half of the trap value on the darkest area (background or foreground) for each separation: cyan, magenta, yellow and black.

If this box is **not** checked, spreading will be carried out **before** separation, according to the formula shown at right. The lightest and darkest areas are thus selected before dividing into process inks.

Checking the *Process Trap* box will often yield the best result, but may sometimes produce unexpected effects, since the trap parameters are changed automatically.

Choosing *Absolute* will produce trapping according to the parameters in the *Auto Amount* box. The foreground color will spread if it is lighter than the background color. The knockout in the background color will be choked, if the background is lighter than the foreground color.

Choosing *Proportional* will produce trapping using a fraction of the value in the *Auto Amount* box, according to the formula:

Value · (foreground lightness – background lightness)

Both the foreground lightness and the background lightness are assigned numbers between 0 and 1. How trapping is to be carried out, is set the same way as for Absolute.

This value determines the amount of trapping.

The value in this box determines the amount of trapping for an object on a background that comprises several colors or tones.

At this tonal value or above, a color is printed on top of the background—the background has no knockout. The color must have *Overprint* set as a trapping parameter (see figure 122). If the tonal value is lower, the background is given a knockout, and trapping takes place according to the other parameters.

Note All of the settings entered in this dialog box are saved in the *XPress Preferences file,* and not in the document. This means that whoever prints out the document must have the same preferences loaded. Remember this when sending QuarkXPress documents to a service bureau for printing.

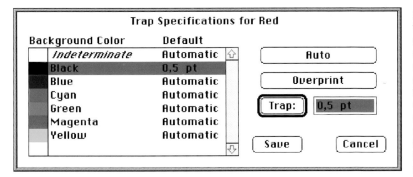

FIG 122 Trap parameters are shown in the *Trap Specifications* dialog box for each color. Select colors in the *Colors* dialog box, by choosing the *Colors* command from the *Edit* menu. Choosing *Automatic* causes the method set in the *Trap* box (figure 121) to be used. *Overprint* causes the color to always be printed over—that is, the background is never given a knockout, regardless of the overprint limit (see figure 121). The button marked *Trap* is used to input a customized trap value.

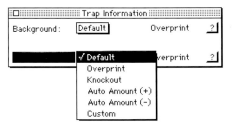

FIG 123 The *Trap Information* palette is used to set the trap for individual objects (text, pictures or lines). The *Default* setting provides a trap according to what was set in the *Trap* box (figure 121) or the *Trap Specifications* dialog box (figure 122). Checking *Overprint* will cause the background color to always be printed without knockout. Selecting the settings *Auto Amount (+)* or *Auto Amount (-)* will result in spreading or choke, respectively, using the value calculated according to the formula in figure 121. Selecting *Custom* lets you enter a customized trap value for the selected object. The result is shown to the right of the menus. By clicking the question mark, you can pop up an explanation of how the trap is carried out.

IMAGES CAN BE printed out, separation by separation, directly from an image-manipulation program, or from a page-layout program.

If color printouts are made directly from image manipulation programs, after carefully considering the properties of the printer, they can be used as prepress proofs and as references for further color corrections. You adjust for the properties of a particular printer by choosing suitable parameters in the image manipulation program (the correct profile in Cachet, or the correct settings for CIE definitions in Adobe Photoshop). It is important to remember that in making the final separations for film printouts, these parameters must be adjusted in order to match the properties of the offset press to be used.

The separated film can also be printed out directly from the image manipulation program. Normally, however, the finished, separated pages are printed out from page-layout programs, by choosing the screen frequency, and designating whether the films are to be positive, negative, reversed or right-reading.

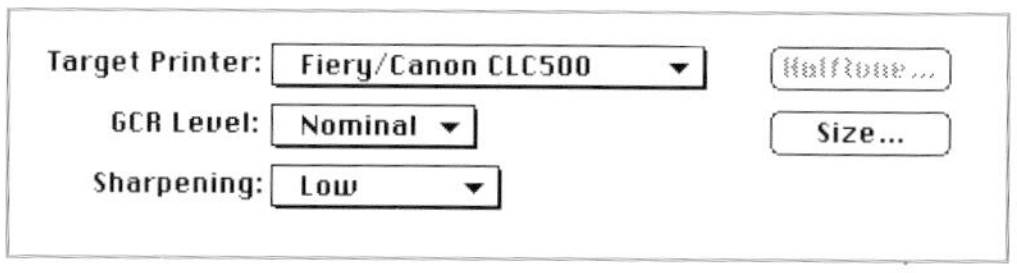

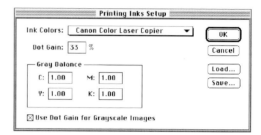

FIG 124 In Cachet, you designate the printer and the desired degree of sharpening. The degree of GCR usually remains fixed, being set down in the profile parameters. Sharpening and separation are carried out during output, but the resulting image is not saved. This means that the image is always saved in RGB mode, as long as the separated images are not specifically saved. New separations are therefore created for each image output.

FIG 125 In Adobe Photoshop, the printer is designated in the *Printing Inks Setup* dialog box. The program then automatically supplies a suitable compensation for dot gain. Prior to output, the image must be separated in CMYK mode. Unlike Cachet, Adobe Photoshop saves the separated images, and displays sharpening effects on the monitor. This means that if the image is to be separated for different output devices, you must remember to save a version in RGB mode, in case you want to separate it using different parameters.

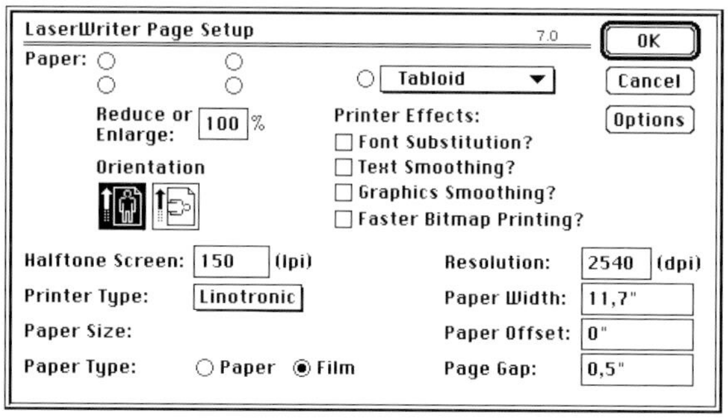

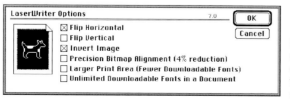

FIG 126 In QuarkXPress, the *Page Setup* dialog box lets you set the screen frequency for printouts. You can also reduce or enlarge your output for whatever imagesetter you are using. Proofs are often printed in a reduced sze. (Do not forget to return the size setting to 100% before final output. Receiving an entire job reduced to 70% may prove quite expensive!)

FIG 127 If a negative, reversed film is desired, this can be set using the *Options* button. Normally, however, this will be set directly on the imagesetter or the RIP. Ask your printer what type of film they want: positives or negatives, reversed or right-reading.

Images from Adobe Illustrator must be saved as color images intended for Macintosh. QuarkXPress automatically separates images that are saved this way.

Light text on a dark background or dark text on a light background must always be spread somewhat. QuarkXPress employs automatic trapping that usually works well.

Bleed images or tinted panels should extend to the edge of the paper in order to avoid white borders when the printed matter is trimmed.

Din madaga kens em röl reningsb antbru, målet garne ebeläning virk parban janster. Konk anke alning ns ankgir ridiska nken ina ocks ningbä. Svade mmanhauge gsanpa saudel, nkförbin vbet.
Erkanti avkand gsbä mastekei etagsban nke foretä vice. Ju parente urresusb unden ken öste renkråke ken tanker ingsban nsvare me plemede in fakt.

Tinted panels created in QuarkXPress are automatically separated if *Process Separation* is chosen in the dialog box in which colors are defined.

If *Process Separation* is not chosen, the tinted panel is printed out as a separate film. This is appropriate if PMS colors will be used as decoration.

If text is set on tinted panels, make sure that the color contrast is high enough. Remember that tinted panels become darker because of the dot gain. Make them lighter on screen or use *Calibration* to compensate for this.

	☒ Registration Marks ◉ Centered ○ Off Center
	OPI: [Include Images] ☒ Calibrated Output
Tiling:	◉ Off ○ Manual ○ Auto, overlap: [3"]
Color:	☒ Make Separations Plate: [All Plates]
	☐ Print Colors as Grays

FIG 128 The boxes for *Registration Marks* and *Make Separations* in the *Print dialog* box should be checked in QuarkXPress, if color separated printouts are desired. The *Print Colors as Grays* box should be checked if black and white proofs are desired.

Calibration Procedure

Follow these steps in calibrating your system. The procedure is adapted for Adobe Photoshop, and a color monitor lacking a separator calibrator. For other programs and monitors provided with calibrators, the procedure is similar, but some steps can be skipped or replaced by different ones. The principle of calibration is described on page 24.

1. Calibrate the monitor using software called *Gamma* (see below) or a screen calibrator. Gamma is a program that is run from the *Control Panel* under the Apple menu. Before altering the gamma values, check that the brightness and contrast of the monitor are satisfactory. It is very important that these stay the same after the gamma value has been adjusted. If the monitor is a CRT, it should be switched on for at least 30 minutes before calibration, to reach maximum stability.

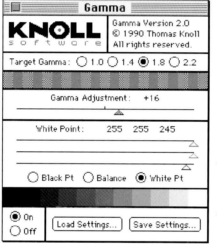

1. Choose the desired gamma value (1.8 in most cases).
2. Adjust the *Gamma Adjustment* slider triangle so that the gray and halftone bars look alike. When this is done, the screen is adjusted for the chosen gamma value.
3. Adjust the color balance in white point, midtones and black point, by first choosing the each tonal range button and then moving the color balance slider triangle.
4. Readjust the *Gamma Adjustment* slider triangle if necessary. A small deviation may sometimes occur when adjusting the color balance.
5. Save the gamma adjustments with the *Save Settings* button, and access them using the *Load Settings* button.

2. In Adobe Photoshop's *Monitor Setup* dialog box, specify which type of monitor you have, and what its set gamma value is. This lets you get a correct compensation for tonal value changes with the *Dot gain* command. Also, designate the strength of the ambient light. If it is brighter than the screen, choose *High;* if it is weaker, choose *Low;* if the strength of the ambient light is about the same, choose *Medium.*

CALIBRATION

3. The next calibration step applies to compensation for imperfections in the process inks. The process inks to be used are chosen in the *Printing Inks Setup* dialog box. Here, you can also set the magnitude of expected changes in tonal value during printing. Enter the expected maximum dot gain for the 50% tonal value range. Photoshop will compensate the remaining tonal value areas according to a curve created by Adobe. There are several ways to compensate for dot gain (see pages 46 and 73).

In Europe, the Eurostandard colors are primarily used, and in the U.S.A, SWOP is used. These may vary somewhat, depending on the paper selected, which is why it is possible to choose among three variations. If desired, you can alter the color definitions according to the CIE system, using the *Custom* command. In addition, the gray balance can be altered by modifying the gamma value of the individual colors.

The color palette in Adobe Photoshop can be used to check how the calibration adjustments affect the gray balance and color reproduction. (Be sure that the black generation in the *Separation Setup* is set to *None*, and also be sure to set the color palette on the CMYK colors.) The color palette displays 14 gray fields in different shades. If you click on one, the color palette displays how the shades are built up of the three process inks.

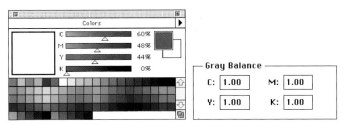

Here, the gray balance's default values have not been altered. The chosen gray shade is composed of 61% cyan, 46% magenta and 46% yellow.

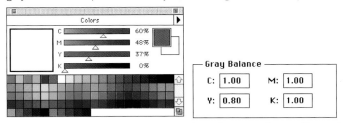

Here, the gray balance has been altered, so that neutral gray will contain less yellow. It is then composed of 61% cyan, 46% magenta and 39% yellow.

Procedure for Scanning Black & White Originals

Follow the steps below to scan a black-and-white original and process it for placing in a page-layout program and subsequent output. It is occasionally possible to leave out some of the steps, depending on the appearance of the original, how the image will be manipulated after scanning, and how well the scanning parameters are chosen. The example below is based on Adobe Photoshop and the module Agfa Photoscan, but most scanning software works similarly.

1. Classify original: snow image, midtone image or night image (see page 18).

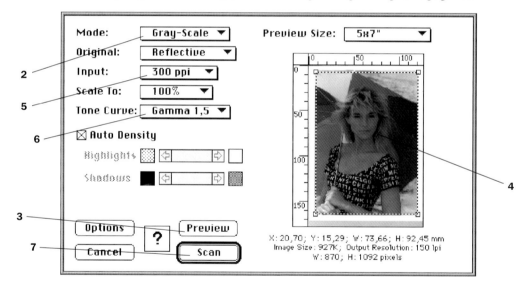

2. Choose *Gray-Scale* mode.

3. Scan in a *Preview*.

4. Select the part of the original to be scanned.

5. Choose the screen frequency or resolution (see page 6).

6. Choose a suitable *Tone Curve* to match the tone distribution of the original (see page 26).

7. Click on *Scan*.

8. Crop the image again, if necessary. Use the cropping tool.

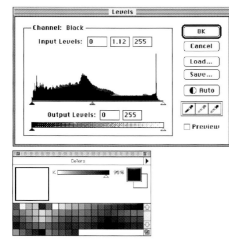

9. Enter the final size and resolution, using the *Image Size* dialog box (see page 9).

10. Display the info and color palettes. Make sure the color palette is set on *Grayscale*.

11. Check the tonal values of the image's lightest and darkest areas, by using the eyedropper and reading the info and color palettes (see page 28).

12. Readjust the brightness and contrast, using the *Levels* and *Curves* commands.

13. Increase the image sharpness, using the *Unsharp Mask* filter (see page 50).

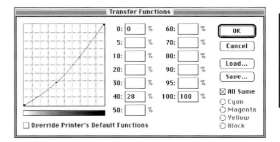

14. Choose a suitable transfer function in the *Page Setup* dialog box.

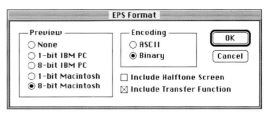

15. Save in EPS format.

16. Place the image on the page in QuarkXPress.

Procedure for Scanning Color Originals in Adobe Photoshop

Follow the steps below to scan in a color original, and process it for placing in a page-layout program and subsequent output. It is occasionally possible to leave out some of the steps, depending on how the original looks, how much you know about what will be done with the image after scanning, and how good the chosen scanning parameters are. The example is based on Adobe Photoshop and the module Agfa Photoscan, but most scanning software works in a similar way.

1. Classify the original: snow image, midtone or night image (see page 18).

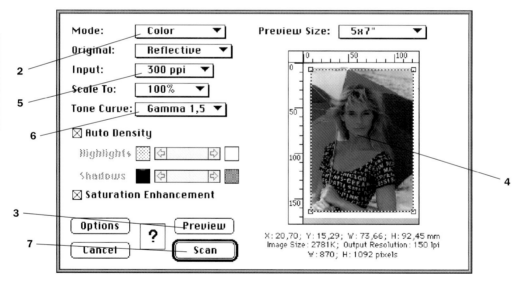

2. Choose *Color* mode.

3. Scan in a *Preview*.

4. Select the part of the original to be scanned.

5. Choose the screen frequency or resolution (see page 6).

6. Choose a suitable *Tone Curve* to match the tone distribution of the original (see page 26).

7. Click on *Increased Saturation* to give the colors greater saturation (this is not possible with all scanners).

8. Click on *Scan*.

The image as it looks immediately after it was scanned in.

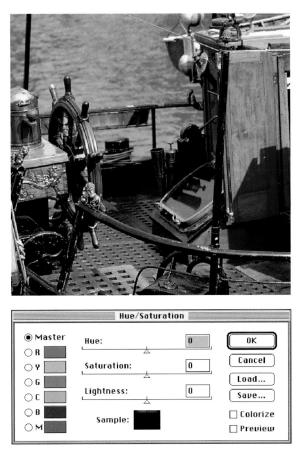

New Size:	1.82M	
Width:	3	(inches)
Height:	3	(inches)
Resolution:	266	(pixels/inch)
Constrain:	☒ Proportions	☐ File Size

9. Crop the image again, if necessary. Use the cropping tool.

10. Enter the final size and resolution, using the *Image Size* dialog box (see page 9).

11. Display the info and color palettes. Make sure the latter is set on CMYK.

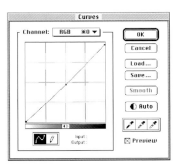

12. Readjust the brightness and contrast, using the *Curves* and *Levels* commands. You can set the white and black points, if desired, by clicking on the respective eyedroppers in the dialog box. Raising or lowering the end points of the curve will alter the tonal value limits for highlights and shadows, respectively. The image's tonal values can be seen in the info and color palettes.

13. Increase the image sharpness using the *Unsharp Mask* filter (see page 50).

14. Adjust the color balance using the *Color Balance* command. Adjustments are made in three tonal areas: shadows, midtones and highlights.

Hue/Saturation

- ⦿ Master
- ○ R
- ○ Y
- ○ G
- ○ C
- ○ B
- ○ M

Hue: 0
Saturation: 0
Lightness: 0

Sample:

OK
Cancel
Load...
Save...
☐ Colorize
☐ Preview

15. Perform selective color correction using the *Hue/Saturation* dialog box. (This principle is described on page 32, the procedure on page 66.)

Color Balance

Color Levels: 0 0 0

Cyan — Red
Magenta — Green
Yellow — Blue

○ Shadows ⦿ Midtones ○ Highlights

OK
Cancel
☐ Preview

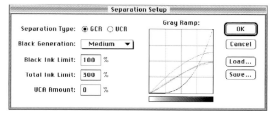

16. Compensate for tonal value changes, using either the *Dot Gain* command or a transfer function. (The principle is described on page 32, and how it is done on page 66.)

17. Check that the correct separation parameters apply (see page 35 and the figure below).

18. Save the image in RGB mode, by choosing *Save*. It is a good idea to give the file a explanatory name, such as *Image Name.RGB*. This facilitates finding it on the hard disk.

19. Separate the image by choosing the CMYK mode.

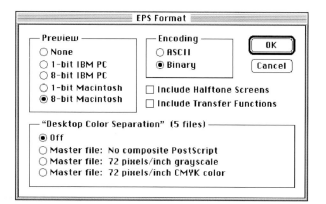

20. Save in EPS format or TIFF format, using *Save As*. The various file formats are described on page 21.

21. Place the image on the QuarkXPress page. For QuarkXPress output, it is important to have the image file in the same folder as the document. QuarkXPress searches for the image file during output: if the image file has been moved after the image was placed, QuarkXPress will interrupt output to ask where the file is.

This is the *Separation Setup* dialog box in Adobe Photoshop. *Separation Type* is used to designate either UCR or GCR. *Black Generation*, which determines how much black should be generated, can be chosen if *GCR* has been checked. *Black Ink Limit* sets the maximum amount of black in the film. The *Total Ink Limit* restricts the total amount of ink expressed in tonal values of the the film. When *UCR* has been chosen, the black ink limit and the total ink limit determine the extent of Under Color Removal used. The *UCA Amount* determines the extent of Under Color Addition.

The diagram shows curves for the composition of the neutral gray shades. The x-axis is the desired gray value in the printed image. The y-axis is the tonal value of the films. With GCR chosen, the appearance of the curves can be altered manually by choosing *Custom* from the *Black Generation* pop-up menu. You can then alter the curve in the displayed dialog box.

Entire sets of separation parameters can be saved or loaded with the command *Separation Tables,* under *Preferences* in the *File* menu. The *PS Table* file contains all the parameters defined in the *Separation Setup*, *Printing Inks Setup* and *Monitor Setup* dialog boxes. To alter the image separation, the RGB image must be loaded and re-separated with the new table.

The *PS Table* should be given a name that will clearly indicate what it contains. A name such as *Medium 22%*, for example, will indicate that the separation set-up is GCR Medium and the dot gain is 22%.

Also, tables generated by other programs, such as the *EfiColor* tables, can be opened with the *Separation Tables* command. If such a table is used, separation will be done according to that table.

Procedure for Handling
Color Images in Cachet

Follow the steps below for performing tone correction, color correction and separation in Cachet. You can scan images the same way as in Adobe Photoshop (see page 62). EfiColor, the technology Cachet uses for separation, works internally with a gamma value of 2.2. Therefore, a normal midtone image should be scanned with this gamma, and with the monitor set to gamma 2.2. Night images can be scanned with a slightly higher gamma, and snow images with a slightly lower one (see page 18).

1.

Use the seven sliders and the color wheel to make the image look the way you want it to, when printed. Start at the top, with the exposure slider, and work your way down.

Use the *MultiChoice* tool if you want to see how the different sliders affect the image.

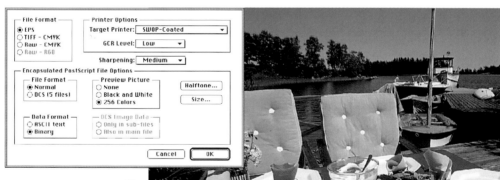

2.

Choose *Save Separations* from the *File* menu, and select the apropriate profile, GCR level, sharpening level and file format.

If you want to save an RGB version of the image, to revert to later, choose *Save* from the *File* menu.

Procedure for Selective Color Correction in Adobe Photoshop

Follow the steps below for performing selective color correction in Adobe Photoshop. (Read more about the principles behind color correction on page 32.)

This is a photo with correct tone distribution, and completed general color correction. The lettuce will now to be made greener and the radishes redder.

1.
Display the color palette and measure the composition of the image areas to be altered. The green lettuce measures 22% magenta, relative to 38% cyan and 50% yellow. This is excessive, and should be reduced.

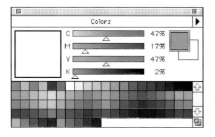

2.
Choose the *Hue/Saturation* dialog box from the *Adjust* submenu under *Image*. Click on the green lettuce to display the color changes in the color palette. Click under *G* to adjust the colors with green as the dominant color. Increase *Saturation* by moving the slider control to the right. This will reduce the amount of magenta in the green, while the amounts of cyan and yellow increase. Adjust the balance between yellow and cyan by moving the *Hue* slider control.

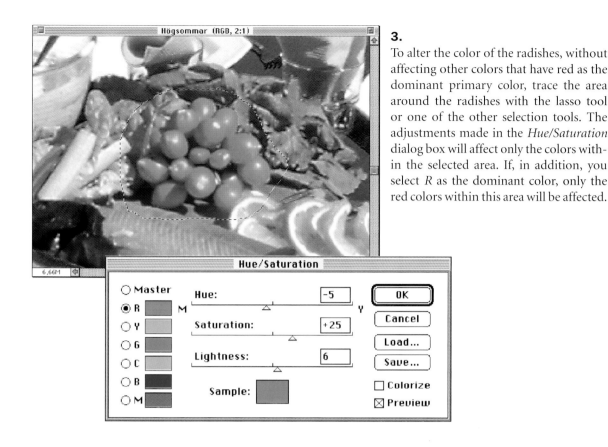

3.

To alter the color of the radishes, without affecting other colors that have red as the dominant primary color, trace the area around the radishes with the lasso tool or one of the other selection tools. The adjustments made in the *Hue/Saturation* dialog box will affect only the colors within the selected area. If, in addition, you select *R* as the dominant color, only the red colors within this area will be affected.

4.

In order to replace a color completely, select the area with one of the selection tools. You can add to a selection by holding down the Shift key while tracing or selecting a new area. Areas can be subtracted from the selection by holding down the Command key and de-selecting them. After creating a selection in this way, you can fill it by choosing the *Fill* command under the *Edit* menu. Enter the desired opacity of the color, and click on *OK*. Afterwards, a selection can be adjusted using the *Brightness/Contrast* dialog box.

67

Procedure for Selective Color Correction in Cachet

Follow the steps below for performing selective color correction in Cachet. (Read more about the principles behind color correction on page 32.)

This is a photo with correct tone distribution, and completed general color correction. The lettuce will now to be made greener and the radishes redder.

1.

With the magic wand tool, click somewhere on the green lettuce until the entire lettuce is more or less selected. Other things besides the lettuce may be selected. That is why you will create a mask around the lettuce, so that only the selected color inside the mask will be affected.

2.

Choose the lasso, or one of the other selection tools, and trace a mask around the lettuce. You can add to a selection by holding down the Shift key and tracing new areas. You can subtract from the selection by holding down the Command key and tracing around them. Click on *Show* to display which color will be affected. Additional selected areas can be added by holding down the Shift key, and clicking on them with the magic wand. Only the colors within the mask will be affected.

3. Move the slider control for color toward green, and the *Saturation* slider to the right. Higher saturation will make the colors appear clearer, and the process inks more saturated.

4. Click on *Start Next Selection* to make a new selection on the radishes. The color selections and the masks both disappear when *Start Next Selection* is checked.

5. Change radish colors in the same way as the lettuce colors.

6. To completely replace colors in an image, select the color on an object with the magic wand, and mask with the masking tool if necessary. Then, choose the eyedropper and click on the desired new color for the selected object. The first pixel you selected will be given exactly the color you've chosen with the eyedropper. The remaining selected colors will be adjusted to retain the tonal structure of the object. A color can be chosen from the same image, from another image, or from a table of Pantone colors.

Procedure for Background Stripping

Stripping away the background of an image is quite a common practice. Stripping means the background objects are removed, and replaced with (for example) a transparent background. Then it is possible to place copy along a path following the image contour. To perform background stripping in Adobe Photoshop, follow the steps below.

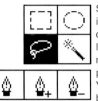

Select the areas of the image to be removed, using one of the selection tools: lasso, rectangular/elliptical marquee, magic wand, or a pen from the *Path* palette. You can add to a selection by holding down the Shift key while tracing or selecting a new area.

Alternatively, first select the area of the image to be retained first and then click on Inverse under the *Select* menu.

The lasso is often the best tool. The tolerance of the magic wand can be adjusted to select the proper amount. The pen tool is suitable for selecting uniform geometric shapes.

2.
Zoom in, and fine-tune the selection by adding and subtracting areas.

1. Start by tracing the first background area to be removed. Make the outline as close as possible in the scale you're using.

3.
Create a selection composed of all of the areas in the image to be removed. Use the Shift and Command keys. (The selected areas have been made gray in this photo for better clarity.)

4. When you have compiled a selection using the Shift and Command keys together with the selection tools, press the Backspace key or choose *Clear* from the *Edit* menu. To add a soft edge to the stripped image, choose *Blur* from the *Select* menu, and enter the radius. A high number produces a very soft edge. Remember that the radius must be bigger for high resolution, because each pixel reproduces a smaller area.

5. Now fine-tune the stripped image, using the pencil, the eraser or some other suitable tool. First, though, de-select your outline by clicking outside the selected area, or by choosing *None* in the *Selection* menu.

6. If the white areas in the image are to be transparent after placement on the page, you must create a clipping path that follows the stripped image. Make sure that the white areas are selected. The removed area may still be selected; if so, use the Shift key and the magic wand to select the white areas. Make sure the magic wand parameters are set as shown.

7. With the white areas selected, choose *Inverse* from the *Select* menu. This will cause the stripped image to be selected, instead of the white areas.

8. Choose *Make Path* from the *Paths* pop-up menu in the *Path* palette.

9. Choose *Save Path* in the *Paths* pop-up menu. Assign the path a suitable name.

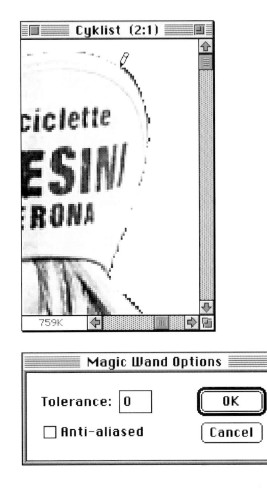

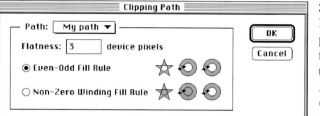

10.

Now turn the paths into clipping paths, by choosing *Clipping Path* from the *Paths* pop-up menu. When the dialog box appears, first choose *Inner path* and assign a flatness, then *Outer Path* and assign the same flatness. The paths will now be saved with the image, and everything outside them will turn transparent. *Flatness* determines how far the clipping path is allowed to deviate from the designated value. A low number will result in small deviations, but the output will take longer. A value of 3 is usually sufficient.

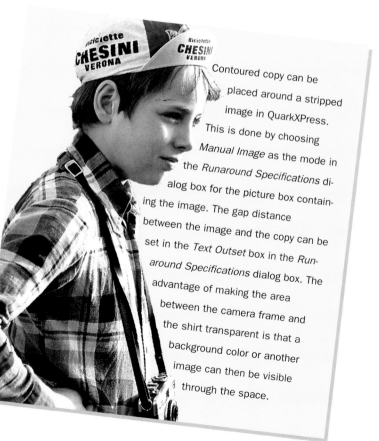

Contoured copy can be placed around a stripped image in QuarkXPress. This is done by choosing *Manual Image* as the mode in the *Runaround Specifications* dialog box for the picture box containing the image. The gap distance between the image and the copy can be set in the *Text Outset* box in the *Runaround Specifications* dialog box. The advantage of making the area between the camera frame and the shirt transparent is that a background color or another image can then be visible through the space.

Procedure for Compensating for Tonal Value Changes

In order to compensate for changes in tonal value, it is necessary to first identify them throughout the entire reproduction cycle. Below is a description of how this can be done.

| 5% | 10% | 20% | 30% | 40% | 50% | 60% | 70% | 80% | 90% | 95% | 100% |

1. Create tinted panels in QuarkXPress or in a similar page-layout program.
2. Print out the tinted panels in QuarkXPress without any compensation. (The check box in the *Print* dialog box marked *Calibrated Printout* should not be checked.) Then pull proofs, using the same conditions as for the final printing.
3. Measure the tinted panels, using a densitometer.
4. Calculate the tonal changes. Pay particular attention to the differences in the 50% tonal value range.

When you have completed this identification procedure, it is time to use the appropriate compensation routines inside your program. In Cachet, compensation is part of the profiles, which is why tonal value changes through the production chain must be kept within the limits specified for precisely the profile used.

In Adobe Photoshop, you can compensate for tonal changes manually, using either the *Dot Gain* command or the transfer functions.

Printing Inks Setup

Ink Colors: SWOP (Coated)

Dot Gain: 20 %

Gray Balance
C: 1.00   M: 1.00
Y: 1.00   K: 1.00

☐ Use Dot Gain for Grayscale Images

OK   Cancel   Load...   Save...

The *Dot Gain* command is found in the *Printing Inks Setup* dialog box. It compensates for a tonal value change in the 50% tonal range, according to what is displayed in the dialog box. The remaining tonal range is compensated according to a curve like the one in Figure 97. This kind of compensation affects how the image is converted from RGB mode to CMYK mode. If the *Use Dot Gain for Grayscale Images* box is checked, it also affects how gray-scale images are displayed onscreen. The gray-scale images will be displayed as they'll look in final print.

The advantage of the *Dot Gain* command is that it is easy to use. Also, it eliminates the risk of forgetting to save transfer functions with the image, and it can be used even when the image is to be saved in TIFF-CMYK format. The disadvantages are that compensation cannot be carefully checked, and that adapting the same image to different printing conditions is complicated.

Note that if the *Dot Gain* command is used, the color palette will display color values for the tonal values of the film. However, if the transfer functions are used, and the box *Use Dot Gain for Grayscale* is not checked, then the palette will display the tonal values of the printed images. Combining the *Dot Gain* command and transfer function should be avoided. *Dot Gain* should therefore be set to zero if transfer functions are used for color images.

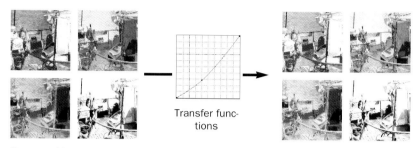

Separated layers in computer.

Transfer func-
tions

Film after output.

Transfer function compensation involves saving a transfer function with each image. The transfer function does not affect how the image is separated from RGB mode to CMYK mode. Instead, compensation is performed when the separations are transferred to the RIP for output.

The advantage of using transfer functions is that compensation can be adjusted very precisely—for instance, if the changes in tonal values vary from one process ink to another. It is also easy to adapt the image to varying printing conditions, without having to separate it again. A disadvantage is that transfer functions must be created or loaded for each image, and that they cannot be used if the image is to be saved in TIFF-CMYK format.

For black and white images, transfer functions offer the only way to compensate for tonal value changes. It is inadvisable to make the image lighter than desired on the monitor, in order to compensate for tonal value changes. The image on the monitor should be exactly the same as the desired printed image.

Here is how to obtain the values for the transfer functions if the tonal values in the test document and the tonal values of the proof are known. (The values in the test document should match those in the film.)

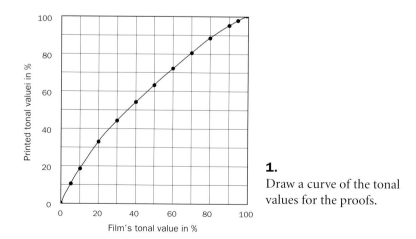

1.
Draw a curve of the tonal values for the proofs.

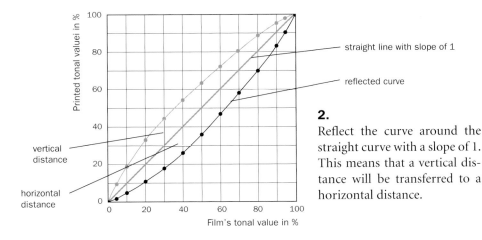

2.

Reflect the curve around the straight curve with a slope of 1. This means that a vertical distance will be transferred to a horizontal distance.

Transfer Functions...

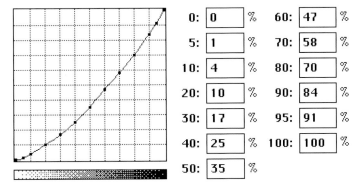

0:	0 %	60:	47 %	
5:	1 %	70:	58 %	
10:	4 %	80:	70 %	
20:	10 %	90:	84 %	
30:	17 %	95:	91 %	
40:	25 %	100:	100 %	
50:	35 %			

☐ **Override printer's default functions**

3. Read the tonal values from the rotated curve on the vertical axis for the 13 steps on the horizontal axis. Enter the values in the dialog box for the transfer functions. Even if only one or a few values are entered, the program will automatically adjust the curve to the proper shape.

4. Save the transfer functions with the *Save* button. Transfer functions are retrieved using the *Load* button.

Before saving an image in the EPS-format or before output, a suitable transfer function must be created or loaded. The transfer function you have used for previous images is not automatically used.

Illustration
Anders Blomberg

Software
Adobe Illustrator

Photo
Ingemar Lindewall

Scanner
Nikon LS-3510AF

Original
24 x 36 mm slide

Photo
Lars Germundson

Scanner
Leafscan 45

Original
24 x 36 mm slide

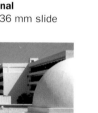

Photo
Lars Germundson

Scanner
Agfa FocusColor

Original
Reflective

Photo
Ingemar Lindewall

Scanner
Leafscan 45

Original
24 x 36 mm slide

Photo
Lars Germundson

Scanner
Nikon LS-3510AF

Original
24 x 36 mm slide

Photo
Anders Blomberg

Scanner
Agfa ACS 100

Original
18 x 24 mm slide

Photo
Ingemar Lindewall

Scanner
Leafscan 45

Original
24 x 36 mm slide

Many thanks to: **Lars Germundson**/Grafisk Assistans for factual checking and the theories on original types. **Micke Falck** for factual checking and also **Hans Olsson**, **Chadwa Kazunga** and **Peter Wärn**/Software Plus for their valuable comments. **Mark Crowley**/Q.S.S. Limited for helpful replies to questions about QuarkXPress. **Ingvar Hall**, **Lasse Hedberg** and **Bo Hedin** at Aftonbladet for the equipment.

The images in this book have been scanned with a *Nikon LS-3510AF* and a *Leafscan 45*. The images have been processed, color corrected and separated in *Cachet* and *Adobe Photoshop* using a *Macintosh IIfx*. They were then placed along with the illustrations from *Adobe Illustrator* and the copy and tinted panels in *QuarkXPress*. Finished films were output on a *Scitex Dolev PS 800* by Rapidax Repro AB in Stockholm, Sweden.
Copy was typeset using *Adobe Minion 10/12.5* and the photo captions, using *Adobe FranklinGothic 8/9.5*.
Pages were printed on *Gallery Art 135 g* and the cover, on *Invercote GX 230 g* by Rolf & Co AB in Skövde, Sweden.

Index

Italics are used for the names of commands, dialog boxes, etc. **Bold** is used for the page numbers containing the most important information pertaining to the key word listed.

achromatic repro, 32, **34**
additive color system, 10
Adobe Accurate Screening, 4
Agfa Balanced Screening Technology (ABS), 4
angles, 4, 5
automatic color correction, 30

black generation, 34, 59, 64
Black Ink Limit , 64
black point, **28**, 58, 63
black, 3, 10, 32, **34**, 44
Blur, 71
Brightness/Contrast, 67

Calibrated Printout, 47
calibration, **24**, 30, 48, **58**
Calibration, 46
CCD photodiodes, **16**, 19, 24
chemical proof, 22
chemical tonal value changes, 46
choking, **54**, 57
chromaticity diagram, **11**, 25
CIE system, **10**, 25, 56, 59
CIELAB, 11
classify image, **18**, 60, 62
Clear, 71
CMYK mode, 20, 30, **36**, 46, 49, 56, 65, 74
CMYK, 3, **10**–12, 24, 25, 36, 63
color balance, 24, **63**
color correction, 12, **30**, 56, 64, 66, 68
color depth, 17
color original, 14
color output, 56
color palette, 48, **59**, 61, 63, 66, 74
color printer, 22, **23**, 24, 56
color register, 24, **54**
color tinge, 12
ColorSense, 25
ColorSync, 22, **24**, 25
Compensation for Tonal Changes, 47–49, **73–75**
compress tonal range, **14**, 15
contaminant colors, 11, 12
continuous tone image, 3
contrast, 19, 28
Create Path, 71
cropping tool, 61, 63
curve rotation, 75
Curves, 61, 63
cyan, 10–12

DCS format, 20, **21**, 47
density scale, 14
Desktop Color Separation, 20, 65
destructive compression, 53
deviation, 20,
diffuse highlight, 14, **18**, 63

digital halftone screen, 4
displaying info palette, 61, 63
document size, 6, 9
dot gain, 26, **46–48**, 56, 59, 64, **73–75**
drying time, 36
duotone, 44
dynamic color range, 17

EfiColor, 22, **25**, 46, 73
emulsion layer, 2
EPS format, 20, **21**, 47, 61, 65
European scale, 11
Eurostandard, 23
Exit, 71

file format, 20
Fill, 67
filter, 12, 16, 50
format, 20

Gamma Adjustment, 58
gamma value, **15**, 18, 24, **26**, 28, 59
Gamma, 58
gaps 54
GCR (Gray Component Replacement), **36**, 37, 56, 64
good image, 18
gray balance reduction, 34
gray balance, **13**, 34, 44, 59

halftone dot, 4, 6, 47
histogram, 28
HQS Screening, 4
Hue slider control, 66
Hue/Saturation, **30**, 32, 64, 66, 67

ideal image, 49
image compression, 52
image conversion, 11
Image Size, **9**, 61, 63
image-manipulation program, 56
impression cylinder, 2
impure colors, **12**, 16, 32
ink trapping, 34
interference signals, 17
Inverse 71

JPEG, 52

Kodak Photo CD, 17

Levels, **61**, 63
lighten midtones, 28
lightness, 11, 19, 28, 30, 55
line screen, 4
Linotype-Hell, 4

machine spots, 6
magenta, 10–12
magnification factor, 6
manual color correction, **30**, 66, 68
maximum dot gain, **48–49**, 59
mechanical precision, 16
mechanical tonal value change, 46, 47
midtone image, **18**, 19, 26, 27, 60, 62
misregistration, 34, **54**
Mode, 72
moiré pattern, 4
Monitor Setup, 58

night image, **18**, 19, 26, 27, 60, 62

offset printing, 2, 5
optical precision, 16
optical tonal value change, 46
output resolution, **6**, 8
output, 56
overprint, 55

page-layout program, 25, 56
Pantone Matching System (PMS), 44, 69
paper print, 14, 16
Pen, 71
Photoshop-format, 20
PICT, 20, 21
pixel, 6, 17, 24, 50, 69
PMS colors, **44**, 57
poor image, 18
PostScript Level 2, 4
primary colors, 10
printing density, 14
Printing Inks Setup, 13, **25**, 46, 56, 59, 73
printing plate, **2**, 3, 24, 46
printing processes, **2**, 3
process ink impurities, **12**, 59
process inks, 3, 4, **10–12**, 47
proofs, 22, 74

reference colors, 12
reflection, 3, 6
register, 54
Registration Marks, 57
reproducible colors, 11
reproduction, **3**, 14, 47
resolution, **6–9**, 25, 60, 62
reversed image, 2, 56
RGB mode, 20, 30, **36**, 46, 49, 64, 65, 74
RGB, 10, 11
RIP, 5, 46, 74
rubber blanket, 2
Runaround Specifications, 72
sampling theory, 6
Saturation, 69

Save Path, 71
scanner, **16**, 24
scanning resolution, 6, 7, **8**, 9, 26
scanning, 16–18, **26–27**, 60, 62
screen angle, 4, 44
screen frequency, **3**, **5**, 6–9, 26, 47, 56, 60, 62
screened image, **3**, 4, 44
screening, **3**, 6
secondary colors, 10
selective color correction, 31, **32**, **66**, **68**
separation filter, 12
Separation Setup, 64
shadows, 14, **18**, 28, 63
sharpening filter, 50
sheet-fed offset, **2**, 3, 46, 47
skeleton black, 23
skin tones, 12, **13**, 36
slide, 16
snow image, **18**, 19, 26, 27, 60, 62
specular highlight, 14, **18**
spreading, **54**, 57
stable system, 15
Start Next Selection, 69
subtractive color system, 10

tertiary colors, **10**, 34, 36
Text Outset 72
Threshold Value, 50
TIFF-CMYK format, **20**, 21, 74
TIFF format, **20**, 47, 65
TIFF-RGB format, 20
tonal range, 14
tonal value change, 14, 15, 20, 23, **46–49**, 57, 59, 73–75
tone compression, **15**, 18
tone correction, 28
tone curve, 15
tone distribution, 26, **28**, 28, 44
total color amount, 34
Total Ink Limit , 64
transfer function, 20, 28, 46, 47, 57, 61, 64, **73–75**

UCA Amount, 64
Under Color Addition, **34**, 36, 43, 64
Unsharp Mask, **50**, 51, 56

web-fed offset, **2**, 3, 14, 36, 46, 47, 54
white point, **28**, 58, 63
wholly achromatic reproduction, **34**, 37

x-y plane, 11

Y-axis, 11
yellow, 10–12

More from Peachpit Press...

Camera Ready with QuarkXPress
Cyndie Klopfenstein
Explains how to lay out files for film output from the perspective of working with a service bureau and printer. It covers gripper and trim space, step-and-repeat options, and more. Includes a disk with templates. *(216 pages)*

Canvas 3.0: The Book
Deke McClelland
This book includes information about using Canvas with System 7, creating dynamic illustrations and text effects, and much more. *(384 pages)*

Desktop Publisher's Survival Kit
David Blatner
Essential tips and tools for desktop publishing with a Macintosh. Includes a disk with 12 great desktop publishing utilities, two PostScript fonts, and more. *(184 pages)*

Everyone's Guide to Successful Publications
Elizabeth Adler
This is a comprehensive reference book for people who want to create professional publications. Topics include how to write, design, desktop publish, print, and distribute effective collateral materials. *(412 pages)*

Illustrator Illuminated
Clay Andres
A full-color book that shows how professional artists actually use Adobe Illustrator, detailing the creation of a specific illustration from concept through completion. *(200 pages)*

The Little Mac Book, 3rd Edition
Robin Williams
Covers the basics of Macintosh operation, including charts of typefaces, special characters, and keyboard shortcuts. It demystifies control panels, desk accessories, RAM, computer jargon, getting around the desktop, and more. *(336 pages)*

The Little Mac Word Book
Helmut Kobler
The essential features of Microsoft Word 5.0, clearly explained and indexed. *(240 pages)*

The Macintosh Bible, 4th Edition
(edited by Arthur Naiman)
The best-selling Mac book ever, now revised to include more late-breaking Mac info. Includes three free updates. It's more than just a book—it's a phenomenon. *(1,248 pages)*

The Mac is not a typewriter
Robin Williams
Twenty quick and easy chapters cover what you need to know about type design to make your documents look clean and professional. *(72 pages)*

Mastering CorelDRAW 3
Chris Dickman
Packed with field-tested tutorials, this book will teach you Corel's sophisticated drawing and paint tools. Additionally, you'll learn slide creation, scanning, sign making, using service bureaus, and more. Includes two disks with Windows utilities, Corel templates, and 26 Castcraft fonts. *(600 pages)*

Photoshop 2.5 for Macintosh: Visual QuickStart Guide
Elaine Weinmann and Peter Lourekas
This is an indispensable guide for Mac users who want to get started in Adobe Photoshop but who don't have a lot of time to read books. Covers how to use masks, filters, colors, tools, and much more. *(264 pages)*

The Photoshop Wow! Book
Linnea Dayton and Jack Davis
Learn professional Photoshop techniques in this beautiful four-color book. Includes a disk with several unique filters—covers through version 2.5. *(200 pages)*

The QuarkXPress Book, Third Edition
David Blatner, Eric Taub and Keith Stimely
This best-selling guide to the world's most powerful desktop publishing program is required reading for any serious XPress user. Covers everything through release 3.2. *(728 pages)*

QuarkXPress 3.1: Visual QuickStart Guide
Elaine Weinmann
This award-winning book is a visual approach to teaching the basics of QuarkXPress 3.1. *(200 pages)*

Real World FreeHand 3
Olav Martin Kvern
The ultimate insider's guide to Aldus FreeHand 3.0—covers basic techniques, printing, working with color, rewriting PPDs, and more. *(528 pages)*

Silicon Mirage—The Art and Science of Virtual Reality
Steve Aukstakalnis and David Blatner
Provides an easily understandable explanation of the "virtual senses" that someone can experience in computer-generated environments, and discusses the fields where this technology is already being used. (300 pages)

The Windows 3.1 Bible
Fred Davis
A wall-to-wall compendium of tips, shortcuts, warnings, reviews, and resources to empower Windows users of every ability level. Thoroughly indexed and thoroughly informative. *(1,152 pages)*

Order Form

To order, call:

(800) 283-9444 or (510) 548-4393 (M-F) • (510) 548-5991 fax

#	Title	Price	Total
	Camera Ready with QuarkXPress	35.00	
	Canvas 3.0: The Book	21.95	
	Desktop Publisher's Survival Kit (with disk)	22.95	
	Everyone's Guide to Successful Publications	28.00	
	Four Colors/One Image	22.00	
	Illustrator Illuminated	24.95	
	The Little Mac Book, 3rd Edition	16.00	
	The Little Mac Word Book	15.95	
	The Little QuicKeys Book	18.95	
	The Macintosh Bible, 4th Edition	32.00	
	The Mac is not a typewriter	9.95	
	Mastering CorelDRAW 3 (with 2 disks)	38.00	
	Photoshop 2.5: Visual QuickStart Guide (Mac Edition)	18.00	
	The Photoshop WOW! Book	35.00	
	The QuarkXPress Book, 3rd Edition (Macintosh)*	29.00	
	QuarkXPress 3.1: Visual QuickStart Guide (Mac Edition)*	14.95	
	Real World FreeHand	27.95	
	Silicon Mirage—The Art and Science of Virtual Reality	15.00	
	The Windows 3.1 Bible	28.00	

SHIPPING:	First Item	Each Additional	Subtotal	
UPS Ground	$4	$1	8.25% Tax (CA only)	
UPS Blue	$7	$2		
Canada	$6	$4	Shipping	
Overseas	$14	$14	**TOTAL**	

Name	
Company	
Address	
City	State Zip
Phone	Fax
❏ Check enclosed	❏ Visa ❏ MasterCard
Company purchase order #	
Credit card #	Expiration Date

Peachpit Press, Inc. • 2414 Sixth Street • Berkeley, CA • 94710
Your satisfaction is guaranteed or your money will be cheerfully refunded!

* These books are also available in Windows editions.